The Care & Feeding
of a
SOCCER PLAYER

By Toni Tickel Branner, MA

Care & Feeding of a Soccer Player

Published by Blue Water Press
Charlotte, North Carolina

First Printing February 2008
Library of Congress Control Number: 2007935844
ISBN 13: 978-0-9796046-2-1
ISBN 10: 0-9796046-2-1

Cover design – Frank Rivera
Illustrations – Frank Foster
Interior design and layout – 1106 Design

Printed in Canada.

A book cannot replace personal guidance from a physician, registered
dietitian, or trained exercise professional. The advice in this book
includes general information based on research and is not designed to
treat any specific disease or condition. All athletes should undergo a
complete physical before embarking on a new sport or training program.

Table of Contents

Foreword

By Paul R. Stricker, MD
Sports Medicine Pediatrician and Olympic Physician
Author of *Sports Success Rx!—Your Child's Prescription for the
Best Experience*

As a sports medicine pediatrician, I have found that many
young athletes are eager to learn about their sport, improve
their technique, find the best coach, and have the newest
equipment to help their performance. Many of them utilize
all of these tools and achieve some benefit. Many of them
realize they need something more—something profound.
Those who understand the value of good nutrition often hit
the jackpot since the body can have all the training tools
in the world, but be unable to perform without excellent
nutrients to supply the body's exercise demands.

I was honored when Toni Branner asked me to contribute the
Foreword to her book, *The Care and Feeding of a Soccer Player.*
Her personal experience, knowledge, and commitment to the
health of young people is exemplary, and a wonderful model
of how to support our children's health without compromise.
The information she provides should be used as tools upon

which to build a great framework of performance benefits. Although the secret of whole food nutrition is not rocket science, its simplicity is also not a quick fix. Sound nutritional habits for the family will not only provide for the current exercise and school needs, but also provide for the long-term health and well-being of your children.

Years ago, it was known how carbohydrates provided useful energy for exercise. Later, science taught us the vital importance of replenishing carbohydrate stores quickly after intense exercise. More recently, research has exposed another important aspect of exercise and sports performance we must control—oxidative stress. Being able to neutralize the harmful chemicals produced with exercise and emotional stress is accomplished with the powerful nutrients in fruits and vegetables. Mothers have been telling us this for years, but now we know a lot more about why certain foods offer so much to the long-term health of our bodies.

Toni's books offer much more than nutritional help—they emphasize that nutrition is just part of the overall picture. Fluids are immensely important, and a well-hydrated athlete is ready for optimal performance. Physical training, adequate rest, and emotional stamina are all required. Supporting your child without pressure is critical, and I appreciate the many aspects of the soccer experience that are covered in these pages. Understanding all of the factors that go into sports activities is the first step to a successful outcome.

Approaching sports and exercise as a family is a great analogy to the "team" on which your young athletes participate. You are all in this together! Everyone can contribute to the better health of the family, whether everyone is involved in soccer or not. So be a team player and enjoy what reading lies ahead.

It's doing all the little things right that adds up to making you a great player. Our first goal is to "rule the yard." This means we should first strive to be the most successful team in our own conference. This will prepare us for state finals and outside rivals.

—Lee Horton
Coach and North Carolina Soccer Hall of Fame Inductee

Athletes are often undernourished, although many of them eat lots of food. They often engage in eating patterns that may provide short-term benefits, but are unhealthy in the long-term. Fortunately, it is possible to enhance sports performance while building, not destroying, health.

—Pamela A. Popper, PhD, ND
From *The Wellness Forum's Guide to Sports Nutrition*

Acknowledgements

I would like to thank the advisors and contributors who helped us with this book. First is my husband, Billy, who is the perfect example of a supportive, but not pushy, parent of young athletes. Thank you to my children, Jenna and Will, who take on any sport or endeavor with enthusiasm and true commitment. I am proud of their leadership and work ethic on their athletic teams. My mother, Becky Brown, taught me about nutrition and the importance of muscle balance and core strength many years before personal trainers and coaches studied them.

Thank you to the many incredible coaches, parents, educators, and soccer athletes who offered encouragement, support, and the opportunity to allow me and my colleagues to get this information to soccer players and their parents.

Thank you, too, to the health professionals who have the courage to teach what we really have to do to prevent disease and achieve optimal health. Just choosing the small fries instead of the large is not enough. This book introduces the newest state of the art research on optimal performance and on preventing disease in the future. Proper physical training can help all athletes, and although a plant-based diet may seem strange, it is not as hard as it seems. The research is very clear, and even very young athletes can understand concepts like oxidative stress and free radical damage.

—Sincerely,
Toni Tickel Branner, MA
Exercise Physiologist and Wellness Consultant

Board of Advisors and Contributors:

Charee Boulter, PhD
Licensed psychologist specializing in eating disorders, performance enhancement, substance abuse prevention, stress management, and mindfulness meditation.

Lee Horton
Varsity Girls and Boys Soccer Coach, Charlotte Latin School, Coach, Charlotte Lady Eagles, College Player, UNC Chapel Hill, North Carolina Soccer Hall of Fame Inductee, Member of South Charlotte Soccer Association.

Lauren B. Lukowski, MS
Soccer Coach and Teacher at The Howard School, Semi-Pro Player, Physical Educator, MS in Sport Health Science.

Tina Marie Mendieta, MS, RD/LDN
Registered dietitian, fitness instructor, and wellness consultant.

Pam Popper, PhD, ND
Naturopathic Physician, Nutritionist, Owner of *The Wellness Forum*.

The Rogers Family—Rob, Genia, Robert, Hunter and Anna
Soccer Family Advisors, Contributors to Surviving and
Thriving as a Soccer Family.

Paul R. Stricker, MD, FAAP
Sports Medicine Pediatrician and Olympic Physician, Past
President of the American Medical Society for Sports Medicine
American Academy of Pediatrics Sports Medicine Council
Consultant for USA Swimming
Author of *Sports Success Rx!—Your Child's Prescription for the
Best Experience.*

Introduction

This book came to be for several reasons. In my twenty years as an exercise physiologist, I have spent many hours teaching seminars and training coaches, athletes, corporate executives, senior citizens, and others who want to improve their performance and prevent disease. I have also spent many hours working with the parents of athletes. As parents, we take our job very seriously. We require the best car seats, regular dental care, and yearly physical check ups. We emphasize the importance of education and study habits so our children can learn how to make a successful life for themselves. We all want to do the right thing but sometimes it isn't clear which path is the correct choice. The United States and other developed nations are experiencing an epidemic of diabetes, obesity, asthma and other diseases in children. It is easier to "follow the herd" to fast food restaurants and send processed convenience foods in the lunchbox. It is easier and more acceptable to take Oreos® and soda to the after-game celebration than to take water, whole-grain bagels, and fruit.

In order to give our children a chance for a healthy future we have to jump back on a path of prevention. The research is very clear. The solution is simple but not always easy. We know exactly what we need to do to maximize athletic performance, optimize healthy growth in young people, and prevent long-term disease. The good news is that the exact same changes that improve soccer and sports performance will also improve focus and memory, lower the risk of cancer and heart disease, reduce the chance of developing eye disease and much more. There is no separate diet or health plan for each of these results. It is exactly the same plan. This book is designed to give the soccer player and the athlete's family the tools to actually put this knowledge into practice.

As I attend games and sporting events, I notice how hard these young people are working but also how poorly they are taking care of themselves. Athletes train for hours pre-season and on the field and push themselves to high levels during games. They deserve the same attention and education about nutrition, muscle care, and sports psychology, as the elite professional athletes receive.

As a sports family we have also learned much about how to make this time investment and financial commitment to athletics work for us in a positive way. Sharing these tips and techniques as well as sharing mistakes we have made along the way may save you some trouble and propel your family forward to a beneficial and fun experience.

This book is for all types of soccer athletes but especially for those who would like to move up to the next level. Beginners, travel team, college bound athletes, or "I'm doing this just for fun" participants will all benefit from the practical advice and strategies. It doesn't matter if you plan or hope to be a professional player. All of the advice in this book will help you grow up to be a healthy and successful adult. Although my husband and I were never professional athletes after college, we were able to accomplish many things in life because of the skills gained through sports. I was a college cheerleader and was able to travel around the country and the world with the University of North Carolina Chapel Hill teams. I know how to organize my time and juggle many projects at once. This is exactly what I had to do with school, chores, and practice when I was a student. I then became the owner of my own company and a professional speaker. I have no problem standing in front of a thousand people to teach a seminar and I owe this to the confidence and performance experience I gained through athletics.

What makes the information in *The Care and Feeding* series of books different from most books on this topic? The most important advantage is that the nutrition and physical training guidelines are based on state of the art research. You want to be healthy now and improve your performance now, but the approach in this book not only gives you the immediate benefits today but also leads you into a lifetime of optimal health. We are just now starting to understand how important a plant-based diet is to current and long-term health and disease prevention. We are just starting to realize that there is no magic pill or supplement that will improve performance and health. It is the total diet—foods working together—that gives the body everything it needs to do its job. It is getting enough rest, training for speed, endurance, agility, and power. It is learning to think positively and focus on success. Starting an athlete on this road at a young age means they will deal with success in life, less illness, less disease, and fewer problems with weight control than the generation before them. Other topics, like reducing dairy consumption, consuming less animal protein, and consuming the recommended daily phytonutrients (from fruits and vegetables) are concepts that are incorporated into the suggestions for healthy eating. Preventing injuries by utilizing proper warm-up and physical training techniques are often neglected areas of education for the young athlete and are explained in these pages. The challenge for players and parents is to study these concepts together and then utilize the recommended resources to continue to learn about wellness and discuss these topics as a family.

You, the soccer fan and dedicated athlete, are the inspiration for *The Care and Feeding of a Soccer Player*. So, get comfortable, take a few minutes to relax and start reading!

1. Soccer: Why Play? The Good, The Bad and the Ugly

I t is important to be passionate about something in your life. It might be art or video games or singing. This book is designed to support and encourage individuals who are passionate about soccer. Whatever your reason for playing or competing, this book can help you reach the next level of achievement.

Failure happens all the time. It happens every day in practice. What makes you better is how you react to it.

—Mia Hamm, US Women's National Team, Olympic and World Cup soccer star

At half time in the State Cup I said this statement a number of times: if you all go out there and leave your hearts on the field…regardless of what the score says, you all will leave winners. You can look back and say I gave it my all and we as a team played one heck of a game.

—Todd Sykes, Coach, Collegiate Player, Semi-Pro Player

Let's start by going over all of the positives. Many people just love to compete. It is fun to set goals and satisfying to work hard to accomplish them. When you win, you can bask in the feeling of accomplishment. When you lose, you can set your sights on new techniques that will make a difference the next time. The important thing is to focus on the process and not the outcome. Win or lose, did you learn something and progress in your skills and knowledge of strategy?

In today's society of couch potatoes and video addicts, playing soccer can be the answer for giving your body the exercise and physical conditioning necessary to maintain your health and to live life to the fullest. You will look better and feel better about yourself. You will have energy to do the mandatory things in your schedule with extra stamina for the fun stuff.

The relationships you build with teammates and coaches are invaluable. Friendships and shared memories are the first things that older athletes talk about when looking back on their middle school, high school and college soccer experiences. You will develop camaraderie with your own teammates, other athletes at your school or travel team, rivals on other teams, fellow sport campers, and the families of these friends.

Today, traveling is a part of most soccer schedules. Whether it is the town one hour away or an event in another state or country, you will develop many social and life skills on these trips. You will meet other athletes with the same drive and focus that you have. In many situations you will see them season after season at the same tournaments. If you go without your parents you will have to exhibit ethical behavior, learn to manage your meals and finances, and practice self-responsibility.

Soccer players have a unique ability to have fun no matter how dire the circumstances. Playing in the rain and mud, dealing with extreme heat, and learning not to take a demanding coach too personally will all come in handy in later life. Athletes also develop a higher tolerance for fatigue and pain. This can be good and bad. You want to be able to push yourself but you should also recognize when the possibility of injury exists.

Athletes need to learn how important it is to take care of their body and health with good nutrition and muscle care. My kids have learned that it takes a lot of planning to do as much as they do without getting run down and sick. It takes effort to pack snacks and a cooler of water before practice. You'll have to get over it when the kids at school tease you about how different your lunch looks compared to their burger and fries. Some of them might even sample and like new, healthier foods because of you. Just a simple thing like making sure you are hydrated, will improve your athletic ability and your focus and performance on the field and at school. You don't get a new body when you get older so now is your chance to learn about healthy eating, warming up, proper training techniques, and stress management.

Occasionally you are faced with some experiences that are not so positive when you participate in sports: unsafe equipment and facilities, coaches who mean well but may not be well trained; a program where the competition is too easy or too hard can increase the chance that injuries will occur and decrease morale on the team. Programs that focus too much on winning and not enough on the skills of individual players and the team are detrimental, as are over-zealous parents who act inappropriately or place excessive pressure on their children and the coaches. In the ugliest of circumstances we have seen parents and spectators who boo the other team and yell at referees.

As a soccer player, you learn how to push yourself to your fullest potential, learn to take criticism as a compliment, and learn to gain confidence from each experience. You feel pain, you experience success, you deal with defeat, and you gain irreplaceable friendships with other athletes. You have something to fall back on when everything else in your life is going wrong. The skills you learn through soccer will never leave you.

What better way to become motivated to practice than getting better at what you do, improving the game and knowing your teammates hold you accountable to make things happen on the field. When you're on a team, at some point you lose yourself and start playing for the rest of your teammates. With the right team dynamics you start working hard for each other and this synergy takes place. It's like you all start fueling each other to have the drive to get better and play harder. There's no better feeling than working hard together in practice and having it all come together during a game. I tell the kids that I coach that it is nothing short of a miracle having a team of 18 from all different backgrounds and at any given time having any 11 players on the field at once during a game reading each other, anticipating the play and simply working together for a common goal. Not always an easy thing to find these days. A high school coach once told us, "It's my hope that you get along during the school day but if you don't... know this... the minute you come out here on the field and cross these lines you're all part of a family, you're one, a team. Your differences among each other are nonexistent when you're on this field." We ended up making it to State that year and it was the last year he coached. It's important for the coach to lead the way, but it's up to the players to listen and make a full commitment.

—Lauren B. Lukowski, MS
Soccer Coach and Teacher at The Howard School, Semi-Pro
Player, Physical Educator, MS in Sport Health Science

The Winning Goal

With hard work, a positive attitude, good training, and the right nutrition you can rise to your fullest potential as a soccer athlete!

2. Developing the Total Soccer Athlete: Fitness Components You Need to Excel

It was once thought that athletes did not need to take time to work on skill training, outside of playing time and regular work. Today, the world of soccer is so physical and competitive that it is now expected that athletes should train for endurance, power, strength, coordination, agility and flexibility in addition to sport-specific activities. Even young athletes will benefit from extra physical training if safety and form are the priority. Prevention of injuries and muscle balance are two of the best reasons to add strength training, core exercises, and focused flexibility to the athlete's regimen. Starting these programs or fine-tuning what you are already doing will help you move up the ladder to the next level.

Let's take a look at the various components of a "fit" soccer player.

Cardiovascular Endurance (Aerobic Fitness)

Soccer requires training both the "aerobic" energy system and the "anaerobic" energy system. Let's start with aerobic. The word aerobic means "with oxygen." Oxygen is necessary to burn the fuels, which produce energy for prolonged activity. By exercising aerobically we initiate physiologic changes, which increase the efficiency of the heart, lungs, and circulatory system. A healthy heart has the ability to supply plenty of oxygen and nutrients to the working muscles during normal activities and sports movement, as well as any emergency situations that might arise. During a two-hour game or practice, it is important that your last play or run is as great as your first. Athletes with aerobic endurance will not falter when they need to make the last second shot or get to the other end of the field in time to make a play. Your high level of cardiovascular fitness will also allow you to maintain full concentration to the very end of the game. It is imperative that this energy system be trained as a base before your soccer season starts.

Aerobic activities are those that are rhythmical, continuous, and involve large muscle groups. Aerobic activities such as walking, running, cycling, swimming, basketball, and aerobic dance increase the heart rate to a target level and maintain it at that level for a certain length of time. In a gym you can use stair climbers, treadmills, elliptical machines, and stationary cycles. Some soccer programs incorporate aerobic conditioning into their practices and some do not. Simply playing soccer is aerobic conditioning all by itself. You can add in your own aerobic conditioning or consult with a personal trainer if you need to supplement your training. In order to get a training effect, you must do regular aerobic activity. It does not help to do a nice jog every couple of weeks. Three to four workouts a week for 30 to 45 minutes are the minimum to maintain aerobic conditioning. Sometimes this is all you have time for and that's okay. During off weeks, during the summer, or on vacation you could add a few more days. For players who are trying to control their weight, going for extra walks or jogs will make a difference. Your coach might incorporate this training into your practice by keeping you moving (keeping your heart rate elevated) the entire time with soccer drills, sprints, and runs. This can be very effective because it is specific aerobic training for your sport.

Anaerobic Fitness

Soccer requires an additional fitness element called "anaerobic" conditioning. This is energy produced with no oxygen. It requires repetitive bursts of high-intensity activity followed by brief rests or decreased intensity. One of the best ways to train is with interval training, which is described in Chapter Four. By increasing the speed, the power, or the resistance to a point where you fatigue in less than 90 seconds and then backing off to recover, you will build upon your base of aerobic endurance and be able to vary the intensity during actual soccer play. Sprinting and running are the main avenues for anaerobic drills but adding in variety like change of direction, ball drills, and agility moves will make the activity more soccer-specific.

Special Note: With any high impact activities like running, jumping rope, or aerobic dance you should wear well-fitted, supportive shoes. Soccer athletes have enough wear and tear on their knees, ankles and feet without going for a run or jumping repetitively in improper footwear.

Muscular Strength and Endurance

Professionals now agree that strength training should be an essential part of a complete soccer training program. Strength is the basis for speed development. A player who performs speed drills without strength has a much higher risk of injury. Optimal agility is impossible without adequate strength and a competitive vertical jump requires developing leg strength first. Muscular strength is the amount of force a muscle can exert or resist for a brief period of time. Research and practical experience tell us that if we stress a muscle or muscle group more than it is normally used to, it will eventually adapt and improve its function. Therefore, certain exercises are designed to increase strength so that we may play soccer with less exertion and less chance of injury. Strength is required for everyday health as well. New research tells us that muscular strengthening exercises play a key part in preventing osteoporosis and preventing decreases in metabolism.

Muscular endurance describes the ability of muscles to sustain repeated contractions or apply sustained force against a fixed object. If having muscular strength allows you to kick the ball once, then having muscular endurance allows you to kick it 50 times in one game. An athlete with poor endurance will be at higher risk of injury especially at the end of practice or a game. Activities such as skill drills, sit-ups, push-ups, raking leaves, shoveling snow, and pushing a lawn mower all require prolonged muscular exertion. Performing more repetitions with a lighter weight or resistance in your training will build muscular endurance. Safe and effective muscle training can be accomplished in practice, or on your own, with the help of a trainer.

Exercises utilizing weight training, calisthenics, and resistance bands will help to increase muscular strength and endurance. Usually three sets of 15 to 25 repetitions of each muscle exercise will accomplish this goal. Variety is important, so switching routines every couple of weeks will keep athletes from reaching a plateau in development. Circuit training (see Chapter Four) actually works well in a practice setting and it is easy to change the stations often to maintain variety.

> I expect my players to come into the season prepared. Conditioning is what prevents injuries.
>
> —Lee Horton
> Coach, Charlotte Latin School, Charlotte Lady Eagles,
> Player, UNC Chapel Hill, North Carolina Soccer Hall of
> Fame Inductee, South Charlotte Soccer Association

Muscular Balance

Athletes can be at higher risk of injury when muscle strength in opposing muscle groups is unequal. Most athletes compensate for weakness by using one side more than the other—their "good" side—either by the position they play, or using their throwing-dominant or kicking-dominant side, so that they end up overusing one side of a muscle group or one side of the body. Individuals often have sufficient strength in some muscle groups but are deficient in others. We use our quadriceps (thigh muscles) every time we kick, walk, run, climb stairs, so our hamstrings (back of the thigh) usually receive no significant exercise during everyday activities. The strong quadriceps and hip flexors pull with more force on the skeletal system, especially the hip, back, and knee. This kind of muscular imbalance is often the source of lower back pain and hip pain and make an athlete more prone to knee and other injuries. This also affects your posture, movement patterns, and can make you more vulnerable to injuries from other reasons. Thus, when using strength training you must concentrate on these weaker muscles to create balance.

A good rule to remember is: stretch the strong muscles and strengthen the weak ones! If you have time, work on all of them. Soccer players actually benefit from a complete strengthening program for the upper and lower body.

Extra Strengthening for These Muscle Groups:

- Rectus abdominis, transverse abdominis, and internal and external obliques (abs).

- Erector spinae (lower back).

- Hamstrings (back of thigh).

- Abductor (outer thigh).

- Rhomboids (upper back).

- Deltoids (top of shoulders).

- Triceps (back of upper arm).

Include These Muscle Groups and Add Extra Stretching:

- Iliopsoas (hip flexors, front of hips).

- Quadriceps (front of thigh).

- Adductors (inner thigh).

- Gastrocnemius (calf muscles).

- Biceps (upper arm).

Functional Strength and Core Stabilization

Exercises, which help prepare you for real-life activities, require functional training. By re-creating the movement patterns you use in your daily activities you become stronger and more prepared for sports, work and recreation. Your mom or dad may only need enough fitness to mow the grass and bring in the groceries but a soccer athlete needs a much higher level to perform successfully without injury. Focusing on coordination, balance, muscular control, power, agility, and the speed of movements are some ways to work on functional fitness. Mimicking the actual movement when you exercise is

a simple way to accomplish this. Try practicing the motions of soccer movements but with weights or bands instead of the ball. Athletes need a lot of abdominal core strength and oblique strength for most of their sport skills but not all of them have it. You can train for this by incorporating twisting and side crunches into a training program. It is also important to evaluate how much flexibility is necessary to excel, and to prevent injury in your specific activities and to train with that goal in mind. For example, a soccer player will be pushed or will fall into many extreme positions which require extraordinary flexibility.

Your core muscles include your abdominal muscles, your back muscles and smaller muscles involved in posture and support of the spine. Athletes should include exercises that focus on keeping the core muscles stable and strong as well as increasing strength during movement. Stability balls and standing exercises are great for improving core strength. Functional training should be used in conjunction with traditional strength training.

Training during soccer season consisted of many conditioning drills. The majority of our running tasks occurred at the end of practice. We would normally be required to run suicides—starting at one end of the field and running to each line and back for the full length of the field. On intense running days we had to run what were called 120s. These consisted of having to run the entire length of the soccer field in 18 seconds or less and we had 30 seconds to jog back to the other side. If everyone didn't make it in 18 seconds we had to keep doing them. The practices were hard but definitely worth it because I rarely became tired during the games.

—Erin Reading
Providence Day School Varsity Soccer, Wake Forest Club Soccer

Flexibility

Flexibility is the range of motion possible around a joint. Stretching exercises are utilized to maintain or increase this range of movement, to help prevent muscle soreness, and to prevent sudden and chronic injuries. This is one of the most important and most neglected components of fitness for the soccer player. Skills like attacking, feinting, and shooting become easier and more fluid with adequate flexibility. Basic skills like sprinting and jumping will be diminished by poor flexibility. Some athletes are naturally very flexible and others have to work much harder to obtain an adequate level. Studies have shown that stretching is most effective when performed at the end of the aerobic or muscular workout, when the muscles are warm all the way to the core. For soccer, it is necessary to stretch gently during the beginning of practice after the circulatory warm-up, but the more intense stretching should be at the end.

Since flexibility is specific to every joint, it is incorrect to refer to flexibility in a general sense, e.g. "Joe has good flexibility." Each joint must be evaluated separately. Another common misconception is to assume that to have good flexibility, a person must have an excessive amount. There are some athletes, who are so flexible that they hyper extend joints and it is difficult to control movement. These players can be more injury-prone. Athletes often place their bodies in positions that stretch muscles and connective tissue beyond the point deemed necessary for normal function. They do this for the sake of competition or aesthetics, which requires special coaching and conditioning to avoid injuries. A well-trained coach or personal trainer will be able to gradually improve and maintain your flexibility level for all joints.

Agility and Coordination

Your soccer training cannot be complete without attention to agility and coordination, although they are not always considered basic fitness components. In soccer this involves learning, controlling, and then using certain movements. Can your feet, hands, eyes, and brain all work together? Most of us begin this training while very young, by hopping, skipping, balancing on a bike, and learning to jump rope. Many new soccer players have to play catch-up in these basic skills before moving on to actual soccer skills. Coaches can add drills during practice to diminish this deficit. It is clear that a great soccer player can coordinate muscle movement (skeletal muscle working with the central nervous system), with quick mental observations and decisions, and practiced technique. Advanced players will practice coordination drills under pressure of time or tight game situations. Reacting to unexpected events is also a skill that can be practiced. Spatial orientation (where you are in relation to your teammates, the ball, and the goal) and kinesthetic awareness (feel for the ball) are also related to coordination level. Speed of reaction and the ability to anticipate are other benefits you will gain with this type of training. Chapter Four offers some strategies for improving agility and coordination.

Body Composition

Your body weight includes the weight of all your muscles, bones, organs, body fluids, and body fat. If the fat is removed, all that remains is your lean body mass. Too much adipose tissue (fat) has been associated with many health risks including heart disease, diabetes, hypertension, arthritis, gall bladder disease, cirrhosis of the liver, hernia, intestinal problems, and sleep disorders. Specific programs for aerobic, strength, and endurance will increase the lean body mass and decrease body fat.

Your percentage of body fat is a much better indicator of your fitness than your weight. Many athletes would be considered overweight according to typical weight charts. However, if we measured their percentage of body fat, it would probably be low or within normal ranges. There are also many thin, sedentary people who weigh very little but have a high percentage of body fat. It would be dangerous for these individuals to lose weight—they must exercise to increase their lean muscle mass. Do not become discouraged if you weigh more than your friends who do not play sports.

Chances are that wonderful muscle of yours just makes you weigh a little more on the scales.

Long-term regular exercise usually decreases body fat but it does not always have an immediate effect on body weight. This is because you are gaining muscle mass as you lose the fat. If you are trying to lose excess weight, do not become discouraged if your weight does not change immediately. Remember that your body composition is improving. If you can imagine the fat cells in your body just hanging out, not needing much (fuel, oxygen, etc.) not doing much—just there. Now picture your muscle cells—constantly using energy, needing huge deliveries of oxygen, and staying very busy. Because lean (muscle) tissue is more metabolically active than fat, you will burn more calories all of the time, even when you are sitting around, studying, or sleeping. Exercise also increases your ability to mobilize and oxidize fat. This enhances weight loss efforts, conserving lean body mass and preventing the regaining of lost body fat. If you are working out a lot and still feel like you need to decrease fat and increase muscle, you might need to focus on the food you are eating. The right exercise and optimal diet are both necessary to achieve optimal body composition.

Body fat varies widely even between fit individuals. We do know that the average person in the United States tends to be overly fat. Women are considered to be obese at a body fat of 32% or higher, men at 25% or higher. Women are considered fit at 21% to 24% body-fat, and men at 14% to 17% although young athletes tend to be much lower. Females who drop below 10% to 13% may cease menstruating. This decreased estrogen level promotes calcium loss from the bones, increasing the risk of fractures and osteoporosis. This is a common problem for those with eating disorders, long distance runners, and other extreme endurance athletes. As a female athlete, if you stop menstruating for more than three months, make sure you consult your doctor. It could be that you are training too hard and/or not eating enough calories.

Having endurance is the key to being a successful soccer player. If you are fit then you don't have to be the fastest guy on the field because in the ninetieth minute when everyone else is tired you will still be able to go strong.

—Rob M., Varsity Soccer Player, Age 17, Charlotte Latin School

The Winning Goal

Understanding the components of fitness will help you meet individual goals and train for your level of soccer competition.

3. Why Warm Up? Circulatory Warm-up and Stretching

Soccer players often make the mistake of equating the words "warm-up" and "stretching." They are not the same and they comprise two separate parts of your pre-training or game routine. Many athletes start practice with a few toe-touches or side-bends. Although stretching exercises should be included before a vigorous activity or your game, the most important goal is to increase the body temperature and to prepare the muscles, connective tissue, and circulatory system to safely accommodate more intense movement. Stretching cold can be more harmful than not stretching at all. A proper warm-up improves performance, allows you to focus, and reduces the chance of injury and muscle soreness.

The warm-up is divided into three parts:

The Circulatory or Thermal Warm-up

The circulatory warm-up should be designed to raise your core temperature and the local temperature of muscles, ligaments, and tendons, to increase blood flow to the working muscles and to increase your rate of breathing. It involves continuous, rhythmic, full-body movement like walking, marching, light jogging, prancing, or hopping. Improved blood flow will bring oxygen and nutrients to your cells and help to remove waste products. Your energy systems are activated to provide more fuel for your muscles and your heart rate starts to increase to accommodate the upcoming strenuous movement. The higher body temperature allows nervous impulses to travel faster which maximizes coordination. In your muscle, the mechanical efficiency of contraction is enhanced so your muscle contractions can be quicker and more forceful.

This warm-up might only last 5 or 10 minutes on a warm day or could take 10 to 15 minutes in a cold environment. Remember that no stretching should be included during this segment. The circulatory warm-up should continue until a light perspiration is present. At this point you should not feel tired or out of breath. Your heart rate and breathing are slightly elevated, your muscles are warmer, and you are ready to begin range of motion warm-ups. Advanced athletes need a longer warm-up than beginners. The more in shape you are and the harder you train, the longer it takes to achieve the same effects from your warm-up.

The Range of Motion Warm-up

The movement in this section is designed to lubricate your joints and prepare them for more intense activity. You should mimic patterns and paths that your body will soon be required to perform. Bend and straighten knees and elbows. Roll your ankles, wrists, shoulders, and torso. Move your body front to back, side to side, and up and down. Go through kicking and changing direction motions without the ball. If your coach does not include this type of warm-up, you may need to arrive early to do this on your own.

The Stretching Warm-up

Now you are warm, your muscles are more elastic and your tendons, ligaments, and other connective tissues are ready to lengthen and stretch. Warm tissues stretch more easily, providing more permanent results and less risk of injury. Equal stretching of each joint will improve your posture and body symmetry, increase range of motion, delay the onset of muscle fatigue, and minimize soreness. Never violently force a stretch. Notice signs that you may be overextending your limits. There is a difference between the discomfort of stretching and actual pain. Some athletes are naturally very flexible and others have to spend much time on this part of their training. If you are trying to improve your flexibility, you might need to warm-up and spend time stretching on your own outside of practice.

Types of Stretching

Ballistic stretching consists of quick, repetitive, bouncing type movements. The momentum can result in damage to muscle and connective tissue and may be responsible for increased muscle soreness. This is not a good method for beginning athletes or for recovery from injuries, but in special circumstances it may help advanced athletes prepare for challenging and vigorous competition. Out of control stretching is never recommended but controlled ballistic stretching can be effective. Go to the point of tension, release and repeat, continually pulling and pushing through the range of motion in a controlled fashion. High-level soccer players probably need some controlled ballistic (contract-relax) stretching to make sure you are prepared for the requirements and aggressive movements of your sport.

Static Stretching involves gradually going into a position of stretch until tension is felt. The position is then held for 10 to 30 seconds or even longer. Since static stretching is more controlled, there is less chance of exceeding the limits of the tissue thereby creating injury. Research shows that after six seconds, a stretch reflex kicks in and allows the muscle to relax. This is why after you hold for a while, you can then stretch a little farther.

Dynamic stretching involves moving slowly and with control through a range of motion. You must have completed a thermal warm-up for this to be safe. Some dynamic stretching is recommended for soccer players.

Contract and Relax methods involve contraction of muscles or muscle groups for 5 to 10 seconds followed by relaxing and stretching with extra pressure. Traditionally, this procedure has been utilized by physical therapists but it can be used very successfully with athletes. Use this method with caution, as some of the positions require a partner, which may increase the risk of overstretching and consequent injury. A great way to learn new techniques is to work with a personal trainer who can help you design a specific stretching program for your flexibility level and specific goals.

Active Isolated Flexibility was developed by Jim Wharton (exercise physiologist) and Phil Wharton (sports therapist) and is performed with a rope. It involves contracting a muscle to relax the targeted muscle in preparation of its stretch. This is a very effective technique but requires proper instruction or use of a video training program.

Many coaches and athletes forget, or run out of time for stretching at the end of practice or the game. Research shows that this is the best time to stretch and gain increased range of motion. The muscles are then warm all the way to the core, and it is safer to push the limits of your flexibility.

The Winning Goal

Warming up and stretching are not the same thing. You must raise your body temperature and increase blood flow. This will rev up your metabolism, improve coordination, and help prevent muscle injury. Stretch only after you are warm and sweating slightly. Remember to also stretch at the very end of practice for the best results.

4. Advanced Training Techniques for the Serious Soccer Athlete

Know the Requirements of Your Sport

Before any athlete begins training intensely, it is important that they understand which components of fitness are necessary for success in their particular sport, playing position, and level of competition.

Here is a checklist for soccer:

Position(s) played _____

Level of competition

❏ Middle school

❏ Travel team/club sports

❏ High school

❏ Collegiate

❏ Olympic level

❏ Professional level

Physical Requirements for Soccer:

Grade yourself so you will know where to focus for improvement.

Place an A, B, C, D, or F beside each skill or attribute based on your current level:

❑ Cardiovascular endurance (keep moving for more than two minutes continuously)

❑ Muscular strength (move or resist heavy objects/high vertical jump)

❑ Muscular endurance (strong, fast movements continually without a break)

❑ Flexibility (large range of movement required)

❑ Agility (quick changes of direction or movement)

❑ Explosive power (jumping and strong, fast movements)

❑ Speed (anaerobic endurance)

❑ Technical skills and accuracy (success depends on accurate execution of technique)

Other Requirements: Grade Yourself!

❑ Mental focus (ability to concentrate for long periods)

❏ Confidence (required to be a leader and role model, take initiative for scoring)

❏ Commitment (long training sessions, grueling game and travel schedule)

❏ Mental toughness (have to endure significant fatigue or discomfort)

❏ Decision making (have to decide quickly where to move, pass, or hit)

❏ Knowledge of strategy

❏ Ability to work as a team member

❏ Control of your emotions (physical contact with other players, decisions of officials, etc.)

Requirements for All Successful Athletes

❏ Proper nutrition

❏ Management of oxidative stress (fruit and vegetable consumption)

❏ Hydration

❏ Adequate rest and sleep

❏ Stress management skills

List your strengths as a high-achieving athlete:

_____

List attributes you wish to improve with additional training:

_____

List the time(s) of the year you need to hit peak performance for your soccer season:

_____

Your coach or personal trainer will help design your training program so you will be at the top of your training program at the right time for competition. This is called "peaking." Many athletes need to peak several times per year or be at their best for an entire season. Ask for help in customizing your training program to assure you will achieve your goals.

Muscle Confusion and Plateaus

Changing your workout routine often and maintaining a variety of training techniques will help you avoid a plateau in your improvement. Once the body becomes used to a routine it is harder to see increases in strength and endurance. Muscle confusion is a technique to counteract this lack of improvement that occurs when muscles adapt to a specific training program. Vary the weight, sets, reps, rest, and exercise angles used during each workout. You can alter your workout every couple of weeks or every workout depending on your goals. This concept is extremely important in soccer since the required physical movements are not always predictable.

> Athletes will find support and encouragement from parents, coaches and teammates alike. But understand this, there is no substitute for hard work, great nutrition and plenty of sleep.
>
> —Adam Ciarla, Certified Personal Trainer,
> Owner of Ciarla Fitness, Inc.

Muscular Strength and Endurance

Safe, well-designed resistance training is not guaranteed to make you a better soccer player, but it will make you faster, stronger and more powerful. It will also reduce your chance of injuries and help you last longer in each game. It will not "bulk" you up or slow you down as long as you are using full range of motion for each exercise and include a flexibility program.

Strength is the force you can apply by using your muscles. Muscular endurance is usually measured by counting the number of times you can perform a movement before fatigue sets in. Both fitness goals can usually be accomplished by resistance training which may include calisthenics using your own body weight (push-ups), and/or weight training with machines, free weights, or resistance bands.

Ideas to Improve Your Skills

The best way to improve is to mark a couple of goals, do 1-on-1 or 2-on-2, just play!

The best way for kids to develop is to get touches with the ball. Find a wall and kick the ball against the wall. In Europe they're called kickboards. You're tracking the flight of the ball and also using skills to control the ball.

A great soccer game is soccer tennis. You get three touches of your body to get the ball over the net. The ball is never allowed to bounce. For younger kids you can modify it by allowing one or two bounces.

—Bill Finneyfrock, Providence Day Varsity Soccer Coach

The following prescription should be used to increase overall strength, endurance, and muscle balance: to focus more on strength, increase the weight and decrease the repetitions; to focus more on endurance, decrease the weight, and increase the repetitions. The American College of Sports Medicine recommends training at least two non-consecutive days per week, although three days would allow faster progress and four is recommended for advanced athletes. Some athletes do weight training every day but they alternate muscle groups. An example would be: on Mon/Wed/Fri—work on arms, chest, and back, and then on Tue/Thur/Sat—work on legs and abs. These suggestions depend on your level of achievement, your goals, and upon the time available. It is crucial to remember to allow recovery time.

General Guidelines:

Sets: Perform 1 to 3 sets with weights or bands. Three sets are optimal especially during the pre-season. You can maintain your strength gains with one set once the season starts.

Repetitions: Begin with 8 repetitions, and work up to 12. This gives you the best mix of strength and endurance. When 12 are easy, increase the weight slightly and go back to 8 repetitions. This way you will continue to increase strength and endurance.

Weight or Resistance: Choose a weight so that you feel the fatigue on the last 3 to 4 repetitions. Young athletes under 14 should stick with fairly light weights and do more repetitions. They can do up to 15 or 20.

Vary Your Workout: Every few weeks or months, change your workout slightly so you will continue to improve. You can change the type of exercise, the number of repetitions, the speed of the contraction, etc. Let your coach or personal trainer help you with a program appropriate for your level and the time of year relative to your season.

Safety Tips for Strength Training:

- Never perform muscle work without completing a circulatory warm-up. Ten minutes of light jogging or fast walking will work.

- Lift weights only with an adult or a qualified spotter present.

- Utilize proper form and body position. If any position or exercise causes discomfort it should be discontinued immediately. The back and the knee are most vulnerable to injury, so avoid locking the knee and never hyperextend (excessively arch) the lower back while lifting weights.

- Slower is better for beginners. Once you have a base of strength and general fitness you can learn to train more for power. Many high-level athletes use too much momentum when weight training or use cheating techniques which are not helpful for soccer players. Try doing super-slow reps for some of your workouts. New studies show significant increases in strength with this method.

• When performing standing exercises, bend your knees and keep the natural arch in your back. This is called the "neutral pelvic position" and keeps your spine in the best position to support weight and movement.

Interval Training

Interval training is a powerful technique for soccer athletes. Soccer requires bursts of energy followed by complete rest or lighter activity, and then the burst is repeated. Interval training is simply alternating the periods of intense activity with intervals of lighter activity during your practices or training sessions. During intense exercise, muscles produce lactic acid, a waste product. Too much lactic acid can make exercise painful and exhausting. By alternating bursts of intense exercise with easier intervals, you'll help reduce the buildup of lactic acid in your muscles. Your body will become more efficient at moving the lactic acid out between bouts of activity.

On the field, interval training can use running, ball handling drills, change of directions drills, and almost anything to accomplish the goal of varying intensity. There is no set length or intensity for the intervals; it is up to your coach, your trainer, or up to you. The only rule is that you must complete a circulatory warm-up and stretching warm-up before you begin.

If you want to do interval training on your own, start with walking. If you're in good shape, you might incorporate short bursts of sprinting into your regular jogs. If you're a beginner, you might alternate jogging with periods of fast walking. For example, if you're walking outdoors, you could sprint between certain mailboxes, trees or other landmarks.

> From a training perspective I typically tell my boys they need to work hard at full speed every day. If you want to achieve the best that you want to be, you need to be dedicated and relentless in your training. Work both feet. If your left foot is weak do not shy away from using it. Come to practice prepared and ready to be fully committed for the next two hours...give me your all and I will give you all I've got. When training you need to train at game speed. Anyone can go out and jog and go through the motions...you need to imagine you are on the field, attack the defense, and take shots after a series of moves.
>
> —Todd Sykes, Coach, Collegiate Player, Semi-Pro Player

Benefits of Interval Training:

- Interval training simulates the variety of intensities required for actual soccer games.

- You'll burn more calories. The more vigorously you exercise, the more calories you'll burn—even if you increase intensity for just a few minutes at a time.

- You'll improve your aerobic and anaerobic capacity. As your cardiovascular fitness improves, you'll be able to exercise longer or with more intensity.

- It adds variety and reduces boredom. Turning up your intensity in short intervals can add variety to your practice.

- You don't need special equipment. You can simply modify your current drills and routines.

Safety Precautions for Interval Training:

Even trained athletes should start slowly when utilizing a new exercise plan. If you rush into a strenuous workout before your body is ready, you may injure your muscles, tendons or ligaments. Instead, start slowly. Try just one or two higher intensity intervals during each workout at first. If you think you're overdoing it, slow down. As your stamina improves, challenge yourself to vary the pace. You may be surprised by the results.

Circuit Training

Circuit training is designed to combine cardiovascular training with strength, endurance, speed, power and agility moves. You can do this on your own, with a trainer, or with your coach and the rest of your team. Set up a series of exercises in a circle. I usually use 6 to 12 stations depending on how many athletes are going to participate and my goal for training them that day. Alternate the aerobic stations with strength and other moves. You can use timed stations or a set number of repetitions. Start each player at a different station. One benefit to this method is that you can work every muscle group and keep your heart rate up the entire workout. You can make your stations either very soccer-specific or more fitness oriented.

Sample Circuit for Soccer Players—do each station continuously for one minute. Two players at each station.

- **Station One:** Sprint and Pass Drill (20 yards apart. Player One sprints with ball to switch positions with Player Two. Pass ball and repeat).

- **Station Two:** Jump Rope for one minute.

- **Station Three:** Players juggle back and forth for one minute.

- **Station Four:** Abdominal Crunches.

- **Station Five:** High knee agility drill through cones.

- **Station Six:** Power Jumps in and out of a hoop.

- **Station Seven:** Dribble through cones and return. Player Two chases Player One.

- **Station Eight:** Up-Up Down-Down footwork drill, on and off a step or box. For 30 seconds, lead with right foot, then for 30 seconds, lead with left foot.

- **Station Nine:** Forward/Side/Backward Drill (Set up cones in a square/Start at 1/Run to 2/Sideways to 3/Run backward to 4/Run to 1 and repeat).

- **Station Ten:** Jump squats (toes turned out).

- **Station Eleven:** Power chest pass to partner with weighted ball.

- **Station Twelve:** Juggling Drills/Foot-Thigh-Head/ Beginners can use a catch in between.

Start over and repeat for a total of three circuits.

Power for the Advanced Athlete

You have a base of strength. Now we want to use that to create the power which is necessary to excel in soccer. We can also improve speed and explosive power to attain overall increases in power. This is needed for almost every soccer skill: quick changes in direction, short sprints, long throw-ins, dives, shots on goal, long punts by the goalie, and any required jumping.

Plyometrics: Training for Explosive Power (Speed/Strength/Agility)

Plyometrics is a method of training for and developing explosive power. Sometimes it is called "speed-strength" training. This is because you are trying to reach your maximum strength in an intense movement and in the shortest period of time. Almost all athletes can benefit, but especially soccer players. We know that the concept of progressive overload (working muscles harder than they are normally accustomed to working) builds strength, endurance, and power. By performing exercises and movements that emphasize strength, speed, and agility and taking them to the point of overload, an athlete should see an improvement in specific skills like leaping, jumping, and lifting. If you choose to add plyometrics to your workouts, make sure that your coach is trained to teach you, or enlist a certified personal trainer to help you develop a program.

Safety is very important because you will be working at a very high intensity. Techniques for jumping, landing, foot placement, and posture are crucial for success. The principle of specificity is very important in plyometrics. Specificity means concentrating on a particular or specific individual or group of muscles, or areas of improvement. Training that mimics the same angles and contractions that you will be using in your performance will also improve neuromuscular skills.

You will experience more muscle soreness with this intense kind of training. The breakdown of muscle tissue and recovery is part of the process of increasing power. So a day of rest between workouts is usually required. Research has shown that young athletes will see improvement with 2 to 3 training sessions per week.

As a coach, it's so important to know your players and the way they think. Knowing how hard you can push them and what they need on a mental level is invaluable when it comes time to training. We physiologically can't turn players into Peles and Mias, but we can make players a better version of themselves. Repetition of individual ball skills and fast footwork spark the development of motor programs. Motor programs form through constant repetition of a motor skill. When a skill is repeated often and mastered, our brain burns that program into its memory bank so that we can physically perform that skill in a fraction of a second with little thought. It becomes automatic and more like a reaction rather than a deliberate thought followed by an action. In sports we often hear a comment like "They make it look so easy," because elite athletes have developed several motor programs making their play look fluid as if their skill is second nature.

—Lauren B. Lukowski, MS
Soccer Coach and Teacher at The Howard School, Semi-Pro Player, Physical Educator, MS in Sport Health Science

Speed Training

Now that you have a strong base of strength, endurance, explosive power, and flexibility it is time to look at the attribute that will set you apart in soccer—speed. Some aspects of this skill are basic like working on your running form to make sure you are efficient in your mechanics. Running in a straight line is rare in soccer so other components must be considered. Skills like being able to react quickly, change direction quickly, and think proactively can make the difference in game situations. You and your coach must decide to set aside time and special drills to develop these skills in the team. A commitment to speed training may be what takes you to the next level.

Other Specific Training Techniques for Athletes

Active-Isolated Strength and Flexibility Programs

These training systems are designed to pinpoint, isolate and strengthen individual muscles. Developed by Jim Wharton (exercise physiologist) and Phil Wharton (sports therapist), these methods reduce your workload by removing tightness, so that you can swing your limbs more freely. These stretches transport oxygen to sore muscles and quickly remove toxins from muscles, so recovery is faster for athletes of all levels. Most of the exercises are practiced with a rope, towel, or light weight with each exercise designed to work or stretch a specific muscle group. I love the attention to the often-neglected ankles, feet, and toes in this program. The best way to learn these techniques is to attend a class or learn from a video (see Recommended Resources).

Pilates

Pilates or "physical mind method" is a series of non-impact exercises designed by Joseph Pilates to develop strength, flexibility, balance, and inner awareness. This method strengthens and lengthens muscles without causing bulk, which is perfect for athletes who need to maintain flexibility, which is almost all of them. Posture, core strength, balance, and circulation will all be improved. The best way to incorporate Pilates into your training is to have a certified instructor visit your team, take a class from a certified instructor, or learn from a video.

Yoga

The term yoga comes from a Sanskrit word which means yoke or union. Yoga postures are used to tone, strengthen and align the body. These postures are performed to make the spine supple and healthy and to promote blood flow to all the organs, glands, and tissues, keeping all the bodily systems healthy. Mentally, yoga uses breathing techniques and meditation to quiet and discipline the mind. Athletes benefit from yoga in many ways. It is a great time to focus on the mind-body connection and to develop better health and fitness in general. A qualified instructor is crucial to making sure your yoga postures are performed with proper technique. Yoga is also great when an athlete is rehabilitating an injury.

Tapering: The Power of Rest

Many soccer-athletes train year round and have several times during the year when they need to hit a "peak performance." Tapering is a training technique designed to reverse the fatigue that occurs during heavy training, without losing any training benefits that you have worked so hard to achieve. It is the final phase of training prior to important competitions and it involves a reduction in training load, by lowering training intensity, frequency and duration.

The word "peaking" is also used in conjunction with the concept of tapering. The period of time required for an optimal taper will vary depending on the athlete, the level of soccer, and the time available between games and tournaments. A taper period that is too long in duration or reduces training volume too rapidly may not provide sufficient training stimulus to prevent losing what you have gained. A taper period that is too short or one that fails to reduce training volume sufficiently will not allow enough time for full physiological and mental recovery.

Here are some benefits of an effective taper:

- More glycogen in the leg muscles (this is also dependent on proper dietary intake).

- Increased density of red blood cells.

- Increased blood plasma.

- Increased enzyme activity in the leg muscles.

- Increased size of muscle fibers (increased strength and power).

- Increased maximal oxygen uptake (better aerobic ability).

- Improvement in the neural system (coordination, reaction time, and agility).

Taper periods range from 4 to 28 days. Shorter tapers are usually necessary when competitions and games are within weeks or days of each other. Research has shown that tapering produces improvements in performance of from 1% to 22%.

A less technical approach to tapering would be to simply pay attention to your sleep habits and your ability to rest between training sessions, practices, and games. When things get too busy and intense, your body will respond with more sickness and signs of over-training. One of the best skills to develop as an athlete is the ability to listen to your body.

Rest restores. The best athletes are the ones who discipline themselves all the way around: fitness, diet and rest. There is nothing worse to watch than a beautiful athlete too tired to deliver. My nephew, a Division One scholarship swimmer, started swimming competitively and daily in the 8th grade. He made his best times after a six-month injury-related rest.

—Mary Yorke Oates
High School and Collegiate Athlete, Basketball and Field
Hockey Coach, Former US Olympic Development Coach

The Winning Goal

You are an athlete. In order for your body to be at its best for games and tournaments, it must first be trained to utilize all of the components of fitness. Power, speed, endurance, strength, coordination, agility, and flexibility all come together to allow you to maximize your skills in game situations.

5. Basic Injury Prevention and Treatment: When To Seek Professional Help

A thletes occasionally have to deal with chronic and acute injuries. They usually have a high pain tolerance and they sometimes ignore small injuries until they become more bothersome with painful symptoms. Coaches should spend a great deal of time on muscle balance, flexibility, posture, and alignment, because excessive tension on joints is the most common cause of chronic injuries. Learning to listen carefully to what your body is telling you is a crucial skill for all athletes. Look for patterns in how your body feels. You might want to keep a journal of which movements cause discomfort or pain. Are you favoring one side over the other? This will help a sports medicine professional diagnose more accurately. Prevention is best, but when injuries do occur you have to adjust your practice schedule and recognize and treat the problem.

> Those who think they have no time for healthy eating
> will sooner or later have to find time for illness.
>
> —Edward Stanley (1826–1893) from *The Conduct of Life*

Daily Checklist for Athlete Injury Prevention, Safety, and Health

• Am I hydrated?

• Have I eaten a small meal recently to provide energy for this activity?

• Have I checked the playing surface for obstacles, sharp objects or stray equipment?

• Do I have the proper shoes for this activity?

• Have I performed a circulatory warm-up to prepare my joints?

• Am I focused and ready to concentrate?

The PRICE Treatment for Sports Injuries

The most important and urgent aspect of this sports injury treatment is the cold element. Several things happen when ice is applied to injured tissue. First, the blood vessels constrict, decreasing blood flow to the area. This reduces bleeding and, therefore, swelling. Cold also acts as an anesthetic, controlling pain and relieving muscle spasms. Ice slows down metabolism around the injury, slowing the release of histamine that increases inflammation and swelling. You can use ice packs, ice baths, or ice massages. Apply as quickly as possible. The formula involves:

PROTECTION: Protect the area from additional injury (maybe a splint or crutches).

REST: Stop immediately when you feel pain.

ICE: Apply ice for 15 minutes several times per day with at least 20 minutes off between applications. Use ice bags, cold packs or even a bag of frozen peas, wrapped in a thin towel, to provide cold to the injured area. Cold can provide short-term pain relief. It also limits swelling by reducing blood flow to the injured area. Limit the ice to 15 minutes. Longer exposure can damage your skin.

COMPRESSION: Firmly wrap the injured area (not too tightly) with elastic (ACE®) or compression bandages. Bandages should reach from the largest area below the injury up to the largest area above the injury. If it starts throbbing, rewrap a little more loosely. Compression limits swelling, which slows down healing, and compression can reduce pain.

ELEVATION: Raise the affected area level with, or slightly above, the heart to encourage blood flow to and from the injury.

Heat should never be applied too soon or it will increase swelling and bleeding into tissues. Within at least 72 hours after the injury, use heat (warm, not hot) to increase blood flow to the area. Oxygen delivery is then increased and waste products are removed. Apply 2 to 3 times a day for 20 to 30 minutes at a time. After two or three days, you can alternate cold with heat (contrast bath)—hot for 1 to 2 minutes (96 to 98 degrees) and then cold (55 to 64 degrees) for 1 to 2 minutes. Repeat several times and finish with cold for five minutes. In all cases, if pain becomes worse or persists for a prolonged period, seek medical attention immediately. Gentle massage and stretching exercises can be added after the acute phase of injury has passed. Proceed slowly upon resuming your activity.

Common Injuries Associated with Sports and Training

Muscle Soreness (Delayed Onset Muscle Soreness)

When muscles break down and repair themselves, the result is a stronger muscle; therefore mild muscle soreness may be a good sign. Muscle soreness usually occurs when you begin a new exercise regimen, perform eccentric contractions (lengthening the muscle), or you change your normal training routine. Attending a camp or practice with a guest coach, or embarking on a new strength training routine will challenge your body in different ways and cause soreness. Microscopic tears in the muscle or connective tissue may require several days of rest for tissue repair and rebuilding. Severe soreness is unnecessary. The key is prevention. Proceed slowly. Start with a smaller number of repetitions and lower intensity, and make sure you warm-up and cool-down properly. Avoid ballistic movements and stretches. If you do become sore, it will usually last 24 to 48 hours regardless of what you do to treat it. Sometimes repeating mild exercise the following day and then performing slow, static stretches will relieve some of the discomfort. Massage and warm baths may also help.

Foot Injuries

The equipment that you use most in athletics is attached to each of your legs. Taking care of your feet is one of the most commonly overlooked aspects of sports training. Common complaints that affect athletes include shoes that rub, tired, aching feet and foot pain. Start with professional fitting of your shoes. Other common foot problems are blisters, corns and calluses, athlete's foot, heel pain, over-pronation, and sesamoiditis. Blisters should not be broken—let them dry out. Try cutting moleskin into a donut shape to protect the blister.

Shin Splints

Inflammation or pain occurring where the muscles and tendons attach to bones can cause pain in the front portion of the lower leg. This can result from running barefoot, poorly fitted shoes, an improper running surface, or from a program which is too intense. An imbalance between the gastrocnemius (calf muscle) and the tibialis anterior (shin muscle) may also contribute to shin problems. Other causes of shin splints include a lowered arch (flat feet), decreased flexibility in the Achilles tendon, irritated membranes, tearing of muscle where it attaches to bone, a hairline or stress fracture of the bone, or other factors. The best treatment is the PRICE treatment. However, stopping the aggravating activity and switching to a low impact activity for a while may allow time for healing while maintaining fitness. See a medical doctor to rule out fractures.

Helpful Hint: You may need supportive inserts for your shoes. This gives the foot and leg more cushioning and arch support.

Knee Problems

Pain in the knee can be very difficult to diagnose. Many times it is the result of overuse, poorly fitted shoes, improper surfaces, or biomechanical problems. Using a proper progression, avoiding uneven surfaces, making sure your muscles are balanced, and not allowing injuries to become chronic will help prevent serious knee problems. Always see a physician and physical therapist if pain persists.

Ankle Problems

Ankle sprains are the most common ankle injury. Prevention includes strengthening exercises, adequate warm-up, proper footwear and ankle bracing. Activities that require quick changes of direction or exercises performed on an uneven surface may increase the chance of sprains. If an ankle injury should occur, the ankle should be iced immediately and medical treatment should be sought.

Helpful Hint: Check your playing field or surface for uneven spots, holes, or debris, which can cause your ankle to turn over.

Achilles Tendonitis

Achilles tendonitis, which is an inflammation of the sheath around the Achilles tendon, can cause severe pain and is a frequent complaint of athletes and distance runners. Usually, improper shoes and lack of flexibility are the culprits, and stretching, or ice and rest, are the treatment.

Side Stitch

This is a sharp pain in the side beneath the ribs. Possible causes for this pain may be an oxygen deficiency, gas pains, and spasms of the diaphragm or an improper warm-up.

Often it will disappear if you lower the intensity of your activity, take slow, deep breaths, or bend toward the stitch and press gently on the painful area. Make sure you are not eating too large a meal, or a meal too high in fat, protein, or sugar before you play, as this will cause cramping.

Heat Injuries

In extremely hot temperatures or high humidity you need to be very careful to avoid heat cramps, heat exhaustion, and heat stroke. Heat cramps are the mildest heat-stress problem. Symptoms include muscle twitches and cramping in the arms, legs, and abdomen. Heat exhaustion is more serious. Symptoms include headache, dizziness, severe fatigue, nausea, low urinary output, and weak and rapid pulse. If you experience any of these symptoms, you should cool off and drink fluids containing potassium. Heat stroke causes hot, dry flushed skin, incoherent behavior, an inability to perspire, and seizures. If not treated, heat stroke can be fatal so medical attention is required immediately. To reduce the risk of heat injuries drink 8 to 10 eight-ounce glasses of water per day and avoid extreme activity in the heat of the day or in an overly hot environment.

The Winning Goal

Training too frequently, too intensely, or for long durations may predispose you to injuries. Never "work through the pain." Learn your body's patterns and imbalances and seek help to correct them. Spend extra time on strength and flexibility. Seek the appropriate treatment from a qualified sports medicine professional or physical therapist.

It doesn't take an arms inspector to spot one of the biggest weapons of mass destruction facing Americans today: it's the school lunch—full of saturated fat, cholesterol and sugar, and devoid of any real nutrition. The acronym for the Standard American Diet is very SAD indeed. We are, SADly, overfed but undernourished.

—Susan Silberstein, PhD, from her book *Hungry for Health*
Director of the Center for Advancement in
Cancer Education, www.beatcancer.org

6. Focus and Mental Preparation for Athletics

—with Charee Boulter, PhD, Psychologist

Performance Anxiety

Most athletes fear they will experience performance anxiety. You might have an image of yourself before a game with butterflies in your stomach, fearing you will fail. Your image might include the spectators laughing or your coach being angry with you. Whatever your mental picture of a failed performance may be, your ability to imagine it helps you to understand why soccer players sometimes experience performance anxiety.

It is important to know that even the best athletes experience anxiety. The key to success is how a player manages his or her anxiety. At the elite level, all of the athletes are highly skilled and talented. They have spent years training and competing. When you see players in action, who appear to be one with the game and who move effortlessly, you know they are well prepared mentally.

Benefits of mental preparation

Stress is a part of life. Learning to manage anxiety as an athlete will help you improve your physical abilities and will help you manage stress in other aspects of your life. Success occurs when an athlete believes in the possibility of greatness in addition to practicing, being dedicated, and having talent.

Here is a list of some of the positive benefits of mental preparation:

- Increased self confidence.

- Improved focus during practice and in games.

- Decreased fear and anxiety.

- Increased enjoyment of your sport.

- Enhanced performance.

- Improved ability to manage stress.

Aspects of mental preparation

Create a positive frame of mind

Your way of thinking, positively or negatively, impacts the outcome of your efforts. When you maintain a positive focus you increase the likelihood of success. Consider the effect of steering while riding a bicycle. You steer in the direction that you want to go. Likewise, positive thinking is "steering" your mind and body in the direction you want to take your sport.

The first step in creating a positive approach is to be aware of your thoughts.

• Notice when you have positive and negative thoughts.

• Notice how you feel when you have positive thoughts.

• Notice how you feel when you have negative thoughts.

Many athletes feel energized and relaxed when they have positive thoughts. Negative thoughts often lead to feeling nervous, stressed, tired, or unmotivated.

The greater the conflict, the more rewarding the outcome.

—James C., High School Athlete, Grade 11

Be aware that both negative and positive thoughts are normal parts of life. The goal of creating a positive mindset is not to remove all negative thoughts. Some of our negative thoughts provide important information that helps us. For example, when preparing a snack, if you notice the food you are about to eat has a strange smell, your thought is, "This food is rotten!" This negative judgment is important and will help you avoid becoming ill. Negative assumptions or thoughts about your abilities or your soccer environment can hurt your performance. If you are struggling and find yourself thinking, "I will never get this. I am so uncoordinated," then your mindset is interfering with your ability to perform the soccer skill.

- Recognize that your thoughts are just thoughts—not predictions of reality.

- Reframe the negative thoughts that interfere with your performance into neutral, descriptive thoughts or challenges.

An example: "I can't run fast enough." When you recognize this is just a thought, you can reframe it and create a positive challenge. "I am aware that I am struggling. I wonder what I can do differently. Maybe this is an opportunity to work with my coach to enhance my speed, power and strength."

By changing how you think about a situation you direct your attention toward your goal. You want to steer your mind's eye (thoughts) in the direction that you ultimately want to go.

Set goals:

Think about what you would ideally like to be doing as a soccer player in 2 to 5 years. Go ahead and dream big. Remember, believing in the possibility is a key ingredient to your success. Write your goals down. Keep this someplace where you can see it. Sometimes we get so busy with daily life that we lose sight of our dreams and settle for less. Even if you don't achieve your dream, you will achieve at higher levels by setting your sights high. If your goal is only one or two steps above your current level you will limit your possibilities.

Look at your 2-to-5-year goals. What do you think is involved in achieving them? Talk to your coach to find out what you need to do. Talk to your parents to see if they can support you in achieving these goals. Make a list of what you need to do and set smaller, intermediate goals.

An example: I want to play soccer in college.

Coach's feedback:

• Improve speed and agility.

• Need to train 3 to 4 hours daily in season.

• Need to maintain conditioning off-season.

• Need to attend summer camps to meet college coaches.

Parents' feedback:

• They are supportive of increased daily practice, if I can still maintain my academic progress and household responsibilities.

• Financially, they can help support summer camp if I raise some of the money.

• They offer their support and suggest that I maintain both athletic and academic goals. They want me to go to college for an education.

Now focus on today and the next six months. It is important
to have goals to guide you today. You should have a few
goals specific to soccer. It is also important to include aspects
of your life that are related, such as getting enough sleep,
eating right, and finding a way to balance time with school,
family, friends and sports.

Examples:

• Stay after team practice for extra strength and flexibility
training three times per week.

• Stop by school office to schedule an appointment within
the next two weeks to talk with the school counselor about
time management to help me maintain my grades while
training more.

• Develop a financial plan with my parents and come up
with ways to raise money to attend summer camp.

• Share my goals and plans with friends. Tell them I plan to
practice more. Schedule quality time with friends to keep
the friendships active while seeing less of each other.

Positive affirmations:

Positive affirmations help you maintain your focus in the
moment. They are short statements you repeat to yourself.
Affirmations can help you manage anxiety and steer your
mind in the direction you want to go. Affirmations are stated

positively, focusing on what you want to achieve. Affirmations are about who you are becoming. They help you build confidence in your current abilities and your potential.

Examples:

• I am good at changing direction.

• My legs are strong.

• My kicks are strong and powerful.

• I am good at seeing the field and my teammates who are open.

• I have a good eye as a goalie.

• My endurance is good throughout the game.

• My teammates look to me as a leader.

• I am confident in my ability to score.

Focus on goals at practice:

Prior to soccer practice, review your short-term goals and affirmations. Make an effort to train as if you were in a game. Practice with the confidence and focus of a professional athlete. It is important to be mentally focused and physically disciplined. The more often you train as if you are competing, the easier it is to make the transition to the playing field. You want to practice with intentions of greatness to train your body to perform during competition.

As a goalie I have learned to stay composed in high-pressure situations. In quite a few tournaments the result came down to penalty kicks. It is the goalie's job to stay calm and focus on the task at hand. I have carried the skill of staying composed from the field into other parts of my life. I feel like having the pressure on me in the goal has made me perform better under pressure in life.

Katie's important notes for being a goalie:

Agility is key. Stay calm, focus on core work, know about your angles in the goal, and communicate with the field players because you can see the whole field.

—Katie G., Age 17 Varsity and Club Soccer Player

Concentration

Some days it can be difficult to focus on soccer. You may have an important test to study for or maybe you had a disagreement with a friend. When you find that your mind is wandering during practice, try to refocus. This may be challenging. Here are some strategies that can help:

- Remind yourself that *now* is time for soccer—you will study when you leave practice.

- Make time to deal with the stressor—time to study, time to talk to your friend.

- Focus on your coach's voice when your mind wanders.

- Focus on your breathing when your mind wanders.

The goal is to bring your attention back to your body and your sport. If you are training and thinking about other aspects of your life, you are not fully focused. In this state you are more likely to get injured. It is important that you deal with the issue creating the distraction. If you use soccer as a place to escape, the issue will not resolve itself.

Visual imagery

Using your imagination to create a perfect performance allows you the opportunity to rehearse mentally. Recall the beginning of the chapter when you imagined how it would feel to fail or have performance anxiety. If you can imagine a mistake and feel the related embarrassment and anxiety, then you can also imagine a perfect performance. Using visual imagery is similar to using positive thinking. It is important to visualize your desired performance. Visual imagery is an important component of mental preparation.

When you imagine your performance, your muscles are activated, therefore, by imagining your peak performance you are priming your muscles to repeat the performance. Many athletes find it is easier to learn how to practice visualization after experiencing Guided Visualization. Ask your coach if she/he knows somebody who can teach you.

You can begin on your own by following these steps to achieve a relaxed state:

• Find a quiet place without distractions.

• Do some deep breathing to help your body relax.

• Focus your mind on the sensations of your body as you breath in and out.

• Notice any muscle tension and try to relax as you exhale.

After relaxing for a few minutes begin visualizing your peak or desired performance. You may view yourself as if you were watching a video. Imagine the movements flowing easily, being one with your sport. You may notice that sometimes as you visualize, you truly feel like you're on the field and experience it from within, rather than as a video. Either form of visualization can be effective.

Begin visualizing a specific aspect of the game, such as dribbling the ball or blocking a goal. You might visualize yourself feeling confident and managing your anxiety prior to or during a game. Use your imagination to help build your confidence in yourself and your athletic abilities.

Anxiety Management

Remember that anxiety is not necessarily good or bad. It is what you do with the experience of anxiety and the intensity of the anxiety that determines how it will affect you. The optimal level of anxiety is often described as excitement or anticipation. At this level, anxiety is motivating. Too much anxiety is experienced as stress, intimidation or fear. You can change your response to heightened anxiety through physical, mental or emotional channels. Try different strategies to determine what works best for you.

Physical:

• Take several deep breaths to gain control of your breathing.

• Imagine you are inhaling confidence and exhaling your fears.

• Get outside and go for a walk.

• Do some gentle stretches and notice how your body feels.

• Take a break and have a snack.

Mental:

- Notice your anxious thoughts.

- Remind yourself that thoughts are only thoughts, not inevitable realities.

- Reframe your thoughts into challenges.

- Break down the situation into manageable components that you can solve.

Our coach always says play to win but don't be afraid to lose. You have to play your game and let the other team adapt to your style of play instead of the other way around.

—Rob M., Varsity Soccer Player, Age 17, Charlotte Latin School

---

Emotional:

- Talk to a friend for support.

- Think of someplace happy and safe that stirs up positive feelings.

- Watch a funny movie—laughter changes your emotional and physical states.

- Do something you know you are good at—creating a positive experience of competence helps counter anxiety.

• Do something to help another person—this takes your
  mind off of your worries and you feel good about helping
  another.

If you find that these strategies do not help you manage
your anxiety, talk to your parents or coach. It may be helpful
to seek out a professional consultation by speaking to a
counselor and/or a medical provider to determine if your
experience is performance anxiety or a more significant
anxiety disorder.

The Winning Goal

Overall, remember
that mental
preparation can
help enhance your
experience as a
soccer player. Being
mentally prepared is
not magical. It does
not take the place
of physical practice and training, injury prevention/
rehabilitation, sound nutrition and adequate sleep. It is a
component of the complete athlete—attending to mind,
body and emotion.

The love of soccer is unending. There have been so many times that I've tried to quit and I just end up going back to playing. It's the comradeship, the way you lose yourself in a game, the stress relief, the way you feel after a game well played, the exhaustion after working hard, the addiction of adrenaline and excitement, those times that you amaze even yourself, stealing the ball from an unsuspecting opponent, reading the play before it happens, clearing the ball out of bounds as it inches its way to your goal line, sending the perfect through ball, reading your teammates' minds and connecting with the ball. It's amazing to me and it always makes me come back for more.

—Lauren B. Lukowski, MS
Soccer Coach and Teacher at The Howard School, Semi-Pro
Player, Physical Educator, MS in Sport Health Science

7. Managing Stress: The Mind-Body Connection

Stress. We all have it. Even athletes. Schoolwork, family issues, boyfriends, girlfriends, not enough sleep, pressure to make good grades, you name it. It can be positive or negative. However, too much of any stress can seriously affect physical and mental well-being. Athletes may have trouble performing at an optimal level until they have dealt with their chronic stress. We now know much more about the "mind-body connection." It has been estimated that 60% to 70% of all diseases are in some way stress-related. Eighty-nine percent of adults report that they experience high stress levels and 75% to 90% of doctor visits are stress-related. To achieve total wellness and to be a great soccer player we must address all aspects of our lives and strive for balance.

> Far better it is to dare mighty things, to win glorious triumphs, even though checkered by failure ... than to rank with those poor spirits who neither enjoy much nor suffer much, because they live in a grey twilight that knows not victory nor defeat.
>
> —Theodore Roosevelt

What Does Stress Do To Your Body? The "Fight or Flight" Syndrome

Immediate Effects:

• Increased breathing rate.

• Increased heart rate and blood pressure.

• Fats and sugars are released into your blood stream.

• Increased blood clotting.

• Increased cortisol (a hormone related to stress).

Long-term Effects:

• Increased cholesterol.

• Increased blood pressure.

• Increased homocysteine (a measure of inflammation).

• Leads to constricted arteries and abnormal heart rhythms.

• Compromised immune system.

• Poor memory.

• Increased drug abuse and alcoholism.

• Increased obesity and overweight.

• Stomach and digestive problems.

• Grinding teeth, nervous habits.

Stress Vulnerability

Recent research has focused on "stress vulnerability." Two people may have the same stressors and problems but one gets sick and one stays well. Why is this? Changing our physical and mental response to the stress can make the difference. Research shows that people who adhere to the following behaviors stay well and develop fewer stress-related diseases. The same things you do to become a better soccer athlete can also protect you from the effects of stress in your life.

• Eat a balanced and nutritious diet.

• Exercise regularly.

• Get plenty of rest and sleep.

• Avoid abuse of alcohol, tobacco, or drugs.

• Organize your life and have a plan for your finances.

• Surround yourself with positive people and friends you can count on in times of stress.

• Take control of situations and make firm commitments to projects you care about.

- Nurture your spiritual life.

- Laugh often—see the humor in every situation.

- Learn to get rid of anger, hostility, and resentment. Get professional help if necessary.

- Focus on concerns that have a solution instead of worrying about things you cannot change.

- Be assertive and make your needs known to others in an honest and polite manner.

- Exercise your brain: read, do puzzles, play games, and visit museums.

- Travel and see the world—go on vacation!

- Be adventurous—keep the creative spark.

- Get a pet—walk a dog whether you have one or not!

- Design your castle—your room should reflect the true you and give you serenity.

- Volunteer—it takes the focus off of you and it helps others.

Soccer, Exercise, and Stress Management

Exercise is one of the best ways to control and reduce the stress in your life. Activity provides a diversion, getting you away from the source of stress to clear your mind and to sort through the problems. Regular exercise makes you look and feel better about yourself. Others will notice your improved self-concept. Physiological changes that occur with long-term, regular activity provide more strength, endurance, and energy to cope with difficult situations. Muscular tension, which builds up throughout a stressful day, is easily released with aerobic activity and stretching.

These physiological changes are also consistent with disease prevention. Exercise can reverse or improve many of the health problems that are related to stress. Benefits can include decreased blood pressure, lowered cholesterol, reduced stress hormones, and improved sleeping patterns. Other benefits can include improvement of depression and mood, and the lowering of body fat, and lower body weight. When you are in the off-season for soccer or have a long vacation, quickly replace your competitive activity with exercise that you enjoy.

Stress Reduction and Relaxation

Mindful Breathing—a simple deep breath or two can promote an immediate relaxation response. Deep breathing should not happen in your chest but in the abdominal area. Your diaphragm will lower and your abdominals will push out. Take time out for sixty seconds when things get tense. Take time to close your eyes and focus on your breathing.

When your To-Do list sneaks into your mind, just go back and focus on your breathing.

Meditation—Follow the instructions for mindful breathing but choose an object or word to focus on. Empty your mind of everything else. Slowly repeat the word mentally, over and over again as you inhale and exhale.

Mental Imagery—During or after the final stretch of your workout or practice, clear your mind and focus on one single image. This could be a shape, a color, your favorite place or anything you associate with quiet and peace. It is simply a "mental vacation." It takes practice to avoid letting your mind wander to other things. Combine this technique with slow, deep breathing.

Visualization—By using mental pictures, you can change attitudes and behaviors. Improve your organizing skills by imagining what your room will look like when it is in order, or improve your posture by imagining puppet strings attached to the top of your head and shoulders.

Progressive Muscle Relaxation—Progressive relaxation trains your muscles to release tension as it builds up instead of storing it throughout the day. Lie in a comfortable position (on your back or on your side with bent knees). Close your eyes. Start by taking several deep, slow breaths. Now, as you breathe in, you are going to tense a muscle or muscle group, and as you exhale let the muscle relax. Focus on how different it feels in the tense state versus the relaxed state.

Follow this sequence:

- Inhale—flex your right foot.

- Exhale—let it relax.

- Inhale—flex your left foot.

- Exhale—let it go.

Repeat with the following contractions, inhaling and exhaling slowly each time.

- Flex your feet and tense your calf muscles.

- Tighten both legs and press them together.

- Tighten the thighs.

- Tighten the buttocks.

- Pull in the abdominal area and flatten the back.

- Tense your chest and shrug the shoulders.

- Clench your fists and press your arms into the floor.

- Close your eyes tightly and contract your jaw and facial muscles.

If you still feel tension in an area, continue contacting and relaxing until the tightness disappears.

- **Massage**—Treat yourself to massage therapy or take turns rubbing your teammates' shoulders after practice. Research demonstrates many valuable health and stress-reducing benefits from massage.

The Winning Goal

Be good to yourself. This is it! You only get one body and one life. Treat them right. Balance your soccer life, school life, friend life and family life. Other stress-reducing tactics include seeking help when you feel overwhelmed, practicing time management, and finding someone you trust to talk to. Seek opportunities that offer personal growth and discovery. Remember that you are special. Focus on relaxation, enjoyment, and health.

8. Time Management for Busy Soccer Players: Notes from Student Athletes

You love sports but you also want to do well in school. So here's the scenario. You have just walked in the door from practice. It is 7:30 pm and you have not been home since that morning when you left for school. This means you probably have to eat, shower, unpack and repack for the next day, do all your homework, and oh yeah, sleep. Here are some tips to keep the stress level to a minimum.

As soon as you get home, eat something healthy and spend some time with your family. As you will learn in the nutrition chapter, it is important to replace the glycogen in your muscles within 30 minutes after your workout or game. Ignore the rumor that you shouldn't eat anything later in the evening because the truth is your tired body needs to replenish itself no matter what time it is.

Assess the homework situation and make a plan. Get your priorities straight and work on the hardest assignments or the ones that matter the most first. It is best if you work on your homework in a semi-uncomfortable place—nowhere near a bed, couch, or pillow. You associate all those things with sleep and you will be tempted to go to sleep right away.

If you start nodding off or your eyelids feel like they weigh fifty pounds each, it is time to call it a night. Your brain will function better on some sleep even if it's not a lot. So set your alarm for as early as you need to. Just make sure you have enough time to accomplish everything. Maybe set two or three alarms!

When you are at school, make use of little pockets of free time to do your homework for the next day, gather research materials, and get extra help from your teachers. Ask for the next week's assignments on Friday so you can get ahead on the weekends. Make sure your teachers know what your soccer schedule is like so if you look sleepy in class they won't take it personally.

Having a boyfriend or girlfriend is sometimes difficult when you are a serious athlete. You have very little time for dates or talking on the phone. This is one thing your parents might like about your busy schedule!

Take a shower. Use this as a time to plan out how much you have to do and how you are going to get it all done. Make a schedule in your mind while your body is relaxing.

Hint: If you have vocabulary words or something to memorize and if your shower door is clear glass, tape the sheet of paper onto the door from the outside so it is facing in. Your schoolwork won't get wet and you won't fall asleep studying. Plus this is a brand new study environment and will help you learn the material better.

Don't waste time! Turn off your computer so MySpace™ and Facebook™ can't use their addictive powers on you. Turn off the sound alarm that tells you when a new email or instant message arrives. This will distract you from your work. Allow yourself 10 minutes to check emails and other computer messages and then resist the urge. Remember the faster you get your work done, the more sleep you get.

If you cannot stop interruptions then go to another room or to the library when you need time alone. Fight for your right to work without distractions.

Divide your To-Do list into Urgent and Non-Urgent, or you can use ABC to prioritize. "A"s are things you have to do tonight, "B"s would be great to finish but you could also work on them tomorrow, "C"s are things you wish you had time to do but they might have to wait for the weekend. You can use colored markers to prioritize items right in your planner while at school. If you don't have a planner, buy one. This is a must for a serious athlete and student.

Break really big projects into smaller chunks of work. Mark the parts of the project off of your list as you finish each one.

Organize your workspace so you can find paper, pencils, note cards, calculator, and reference books quickly and without wasting time.

If you have appointments or breaks in your soccer or school schedule, always have reading material or notes to study. Little pockets of time can really add up.

Know yourself. If you know you can't resist looking at your cell phone every two minutes to see your text messages and missed calls—leave it in the laundry room or the garage until your work is finished. If you know you work better after a snack then take time to eat and then get to work. Are you a morning person or a night owl? Do you like to study in groups or by yourself? The more you know about yourself the more efficient and effective you can be.

When your parents see your good grades they will be much more supportive of your soccer commitments.

A Piece of My Life: Soccer
By: Taylor R. Age 16

(I dedicate this to my girls on the U-17 RSL soccer team!)

She brings it up the middle, crosses it over, plays it outside down the line, across in the box, and… GOAL!!!! These words are what every teenage soccer player loves to hear.

The relief that her team was able to put one in the goal—the reward from all the training before the game, and finally the joy of succeeding in the sport you love most. But soccer is not just a sport; it's part of my life. Soccer is a lifestyle that involves friendships, building character, and love.

I dedicate 6 hours a week along with 4 to 5 hours, if not more, every weekend to soccer. It definitely dictates my lifestyle. On top of the time commitment, I have to prepare myself on my own to be able to perform my best every day on the field. This involves maintaining fitness and staying in shape, eating healthy, nutritious meals, and staying out of the trouble a lot of teenagers partake in. Soccer teaches you time management along with dedication. Being prompt to practice is always important. You also have to make sacrifices with your social life. This dedication to a sport prepares you for commitments later on in life.

Despite the sacrifices made, I am still able to maintain a social life, especially with my team. The girls on my team are a family. We go out together and have a blast. I enjoy going to tournaments for the whole weekend because I know I will have fun with my team. If one of the girls has a test for school that next week, we'll help her study. Not only are the girls on my team extremely close, but the coaches and parents are too. Our team went to Universal Studios together and filmed a music video. Another time we went to Halloween Horror Nights. The coaches serve as great role models for us. I've even had deep talks about religion with one of my coaches. The parents love getting together and going out to dinner at our tournaments. These bonds of friendship have even helped me adjust through a move. When I moved from Indiana to Tampa, I immediately tried out for a club soccer team. Soccer was my first connection to Tampa—I automatically had 16 friends!

Along with learning about the bonds of friendship, soccer teaches you how to build strong character that helps you through life. Being a team sport, soccer offers interaction with more people to further develop your character. Soccer teaches you commitment not only to the sport, but also to every one of your teammates. If you make a mistake or make a poor choice, you let your whole team down, and you have to be ready to take that responsibility. Soccer also teaches discipline; the discipline needed to go out and push yourself at every practice. It also includes the discipline to stay out of trouble, so you don't let your team down. Because soccer is a team sport, I have enhanced my leadership skills significantly. Being one of the captains of the team, it is my responsibility to look out for each of them—keep them out of trouble and lead them on the field. It's my job to talk, talk, talk. If we get scored on, I have to get the team focused and not let down. This role of leadership carries over in life and being successful. Soccer teaches a player respect as well. They learn respect for their coaches and parents most of all. They recognize how much these adults do for them and they gain respect for their love toward them. Players also learn respect for the other team and for the game of soccer. The respect for the other team is shown on the field through good sportsmanship. The other team trains just like we do, and no matter whether we win or lose, we respect their hard work. The respect for game is modeled by listening to the referee's calls. Another life lesson happens when the ref makes an unfavorable call; you have to let it go, just like the curveballs in life. And lastly, soccer teaches time management. Balancing schoolwork, practices, friends, family, faith and even finding time to shower and eat takes a lot of preparation. You have to know what time practice starts and what homework you have to get done beforehand. Instead of going to eat with your friends after school, you might have to go to the library and do your homework. This characteristic is very useful later on in life.

You might wonder what does love have to do with playing a sport? But soccer, especially at the highly competitive level I play, is dictated by love. Considering how much time you spend with them, you have to love your team. Love on a team is reflected on the field: the way you train, the way you win or lose, and finally the way you treat each other. You must also have love for the sport. My love for soccer and my team makes it twice as easy to sacrifice some of my social life. I love the game of soccer; therefore I am willing to train and push myself to be better. In addition to the love for soccer, this sport teaches you to love yourself. You learn how to live a healthy lifestyle and respect your body and physical limits. If something hurts, it's your job to let the coach know and properly take care of it. Lastly, you gain even more love for your parents. Soccer helps you realize how much your parents sacrifice for you. Their love for you is shown by their driving you to practice and by spending an exorbitant amount of money on uniforms, cleats, team dues, tournaments, etc. From love to building character, soccer is more than just a sport.

I can't imagine not playing soccer. If I didn't play soccer, my life would be dull and slow. I love the constant busyness, and I love the valuable lessons soccer teaches me that will benefit me later on in life. Being a student-athlete helps me learn how to take care of myself and provide a sturdy foundation for my values. Soccer is more than just a sport; it's a part of my life.

The Winning Goal

Spend your precious time on things that truly are important and can make a difference. Good grades, becoming a better athlete, getting enough sleep, and spending time with your family or a friend are all worthwhile and will have a lasting benefit. Watching TV, instant messaging and surfing the Internet may have to wait!

9. Oxidative Stress and Free Radicals: Why Soccer Players Need Fruits and Veggies

After a long practice or game you feel tired but good. Although you are working hard and getting stronger and more flexible, there is also something going on inside your cells. The very oxygen that you breathe is attacking your cells. Chemical reactions in your body produce oxidants, which are called free radicals. These free radicals are missing an electron, which makes them very unstable. They run around your body trying to "steal" an electron from your healthy molecules. This can cause damage to cell membranes, red blood cells, muscle fibers, proteins and even your DNA (your blueprint to make more cells). The free radicals cause a chain reaction of destruction to your cells. By attacking cell membranes, they cause cellular damage, muscle fatigue, injury and vulnerability to chronic disease. Everyone experiences oxidative stress but athletes and people who exercise strenuously have excessive amounts. As intensity and duration increase—oxidative damage increases. So while exercise and soccer are good for you, you need to prevent long-term damage by eating the right foods (antioxidants and phytonutrients) to stabilize and stop the free radical damage.

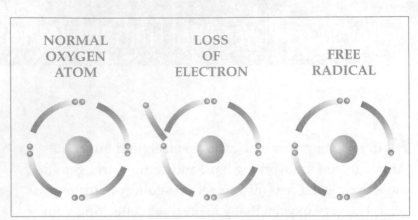

NORMAL OXYGEN ATOM   LOSS OF ELECTRON   FREE RADICAL

You produce billions of free radicals per day, per cell in your body. They are missing an electron so they are unstable and can cause damage to healthy molecules in your body. Athletes produce more free radicals than other people. Your food choices will help you stop these free radicals in their tracks before damage occurs.

Some diseases linked by research to oxidative stress:

Cardiovascular disease	*Alzheimer's disease*
Cancer	*Parkinson's disease*
Lung disease	*Cataracts*
Macular degeneration (eyes)	*Poor immune system*
Diabetes	*Wrinkling and skin damage*
Arthritis	

Other factors in the production of free radicals and oxidative stress:

Alcohol consumption	*Sickness and injury*
UV light from the sun	*Toxins in the environment*
Psychological stress (Taking the SAT!)	*Smoking or second hand smoke*

How to Eat the Right Foods to Get Antioxidants and Phytonutrients

There are thousands of nutrients and live enzymes in fruits, vegetables, nuts, seeds, beans, and grains. These are called "phytochemicals" or "phytonutrients." We will call them "phytos" for short. There are different ones in each color of fruits and vegetables. So broccoli has different phytos than sweet potatoes or blueberries. These phytos have all the antioxidants you need to neutralize the free radicals and slow damage to your body. Both the best research and our government recommend that you include 9 to 13 raw fruits and vegetables in your diet every day. This is what it takes to prevent disease, reduce damage to your proteins and DNA, and build your immune system. Isolated, man-made vitamins have not been found to be as effective in lowering oxidative stress except in higher toxic doses, e.g. side effects like kidney damage. You must get antioxidants and phytos from your food. Each color of fruits and vegetables has different nutrients, and they all have important roles in human nutrition and in maintaining health. One apple has over ten thousand identified phytos. These nutrients work in a delicate balance to perform all of the important functions in the cells of your body. You cannot get this from a man-made vitamin pill. If you know you don't eat the recommended amount

every day, try a whole food supplement that is actually made from real juiced fruits and vegetables. See the next chapter and the Recommended Resources for information on Juice Plus+® which is the product I recommend to my clients. Choose fruits and vegetables with a lot of color: dark green, purple and blue, deep orange and red and don't forget the nuts, seeds and whole-grains.

Athletes Should Eat the Rainbow Every Day!

According to the government's New Food Guide Pyramid, teenage athletes need thirteen different colors of raw fruits and veggies every single day.

Blue and Purple—Great at Stopping Those Free Radicals!

Blackberries

Blueberries

Black currants

Dried plums

Elderberries

Purple figs

Purple grapes

Plums

Raisins

Purple asparagus

Purple cabbage

Purple carrots

Eggplant

Purple Belgian endive

Purple peppers

Potatoes (purple fleshed)

Black salsify

Go for the Green!—Lowers risk of cancer, protects your vision, and builds strong bones and teeth.

Avocados

Green apples

Green grapes

Honeydew

Kiwi

Limes

Green pears

Artichokes

Arugula

Asparagus

Broccoflower

Broccoli

Broccoli rabe

Brussels sprouts

Chinese cabbage

Green beans

Green cabbage

Celery

Chayote squash

Cucumbers

Endive

Leafy greens

Leeks

Lettuce

Green onion

Okra

Peas

Green pepper

Snow Peas

Sugar snap peas

Spinach

Watercress

Zucchini

WHITE is Right!—Good for your heart and lowers cancer risk.

Bananas	*Jicama*
Brown pears	*Kohlrabi*
Dates	*Mushrooms*
White nectarines	*Onions*
White peaches	*Parsnips*
Cauliflower	*Potatoes (white fleshed)*
Garlic	*Shallots*
Ginger	*Turnips*
Jerusalem artichoke	*White Corn*

YELLOW and ORANGE—Builds your immune system and improves health in every way.

Yellow apples	*Mangoes*
Apricots	*Nectarines*
Cantaloupe	*Oranges*
Cape gooseberries	*Papayas*
Yellow figs	*Peaches*
Grapefruit	*Yellow pears*
Golden kiwi	*Persimmons*
Lemon	*Pineapples*

Tangerines
Yellow watermelon
Yellow beets
Butternut squash
Carrots
Yellow peppers
Yellow potatoes
Pumpkin

Rutabagas
Yellow summer squash
Sweet corn
Sweet potatoes
Yellow tomatoes
Yellow winter squash

I SAID RED—Helps you remember things, prevents urinary tract problems, and protects your heart.

Red apples
Blood oranges
Cherries
Cranberries
Red grapes
Pink/Red grapefruit
Red pears
Pomegranates
Raspberries
Strawberries

Watermelon

Beets
Red peppers
Radishes
Radicchio
Red onions
Red potatoes
Rhubarb
Tomatoes

10 Ways Soccer Players Can Eat More Fruits and Veggies:

1. Pack dried fruit like raisins, apricots, and figs in small bags with raw almonds in your soccer bag.

2. Make a fruit or chocolate banana smoothie for breakfast or after practice.

3. Cut up veggies and make healthy dip on the weekend so you can grab-and-go all week!

4. Keep a big bowl of apples, pears, and oranges on the counter to throw in your lunch or your gym bag for school or practice. No packaging required!

5. Always eat fruit on your cereal (whole-grain is best).

6. Order sides of veggies in restaurants. Almost all restaurants will bring you a side of broccoli (skip the cheese sauce) or green beans.

7. See how colorful you can make your salad. Try for at least five different colors of veggies. Croutons and Bacon Bits® don't count!

8. Learn to eat food with beans. Put beans on your salad. Rice and beans and Mexican dishes are delicious!

Fruits and vegetables get their colors from carotenoids, a large group of 600 or so natural plant chemicals. Carotenes play two enormous roles in our health. First they boost immune function. Secondly, the carotenes are powerful antioxidants, essential for quenching free radicals. The one color God put on this planet more than any other is the color green. Chlorophyll is one of the most powerful wound healers and blood-builders known. We should be consuming vegetables that are as dark green as possible every day. They are actually higher in bioavailable calcium than dairy products, with a perfect ratio of calcium and magnesium.

—Susan Silberstein, PhD, from her book *Hungry for Health*
Director of the Center for Advancement in
Cancer Education, www.beatcancer.org

9. Try 100% fruit juice instead of soda or other sugary drinks. Orange juice with calcium and vitamin D is a great choice but the real fruit is even better because it has the fiber intact.

10. Fresh pineapple has an enzyme that repairs muscle—a great snack after a hard practice or game.

When dealing with the pressures of training and competition, it is important to know there are many variables that affect performance, such as genetics, development, and emotional maturity. Yet nutrition is a major component that is too often overlooked for its benefits of providing energy and chemical protection for optimal performance.

—Paul Stricker, MD, FAAP
Sports Medicine Pediatrician and Olympic Physician
From his book *Sports Success Rx!*

The Winning Goal

Healthy eating and reducing oxidative stress is all about color and phytonutrients from fruits and vegetables. Your Plate Should Look Like a Rainbow!

10. Whole Food Nutrition for Soccer Players and their Families

The right diet can enhance your performance as an athlete and as a student and can help you lead a long and happy life. The real news is not that a healthy diet is good for you— we all know that—the real news is that a healthy diet may save your life. From the last chapter we now know that consuming a variety of the right foods lowers a person's risk for many chronic diseases and enhances the benefits gained through regular exercise and sports training. Sport-specific

> Your caloric intake is directly linked to performance, recovery, normal growth and development, and body weight goals. The young athlete has nutritional requirements that are greater than average people. These requirements can be met by eating 5 to 7 small, nutrient-dense meals throughout the day. Make sure you follow a sports-specific nutrition program, consume enough calories, and get adequate periods of rest and recovery. Remember, NO PAIN, NO GAIN and TRAIN UNTIL YOU DROP is for fools.
>
> —From *PowerPack for the Winning Edge*, by Jack A. Medina, MA and Roy E. Vartabedian, PhD

workouts and exercise sessions, combined with proper nutrition, will aid in weight control, help reduce calcium loss from bones, and reduce the negative effects of stress and anxiety. No matter what your personal goals for sports may be, a nutrition plan is essential.

It can be difficult to make these changes when most of your friends are feasting on fast food and pizza. It takes discipline and planning to eat an optimal diet day in and day out. The good news is that the same dietary changes that make you a better soccer player will also build your immune system and protect you from illness and disease. A few carefully made changes can modify your nutritional habits for a lifetime of optimal health and maximal performance.

What Should I Eat?

All individuals should consume a plant-based diet with about 65% to 70% of calories from carbohydrates, 15% of calories from protein and 15% to 20% from fat. Athletes simply need more calories than the average person because of their activity level. The proportion of each nutrient in the diet remains the same, so the entire family can make these changes together. The research is very clear that the same dietary choices that prevent cancer and heart disease also reduce your risk of obesity, eye disease, Alzheimer's disease, Parkinson's disease and many other lifestyle-related

diseases. The changes are not all easy but they are simple.
If your favorite food is high in fat and sugar you will need
to save it for very special occasions or perhaps decrease the
quantity. If you really savor the taste you may not need such
a large portion. Go for quality—not quantity!

The information in this book is intended as a general
guideline for the athlete and the rest of the family. If you
have any medical conditions or are taking any medications
it is important to consult a registered dietitian and your
physician for specific advice.

Carbohydrates

Carbohydrates are the most important nutrient for exercising
muscles and they are also needed for optimal brain and
central nervous system function. The recommended amount
of carbohydrate for athletes is 65% to 70% of your total
caloric intake. Carbohydrates are necessary nutrients but it
is important to consume the right kind. Refined sugars and
starches like white bread, sodas, cookies, donuts, and candy
have little nutritional value and are quickly absorbed and
stored as fat. Because these sugary foods are digested so
quickly they overload the blood with glucose.

Complex carbohydrates are foods that are left in their whole
state such as whole-grains, fruits, vegetables, and legumes
(beans). They still have the vitamins, minerals and fiber

intact and they take much longer to be broken down. Their sugars are released much more slowly into the bloodstream avoiding excess glucose in the blood.

How Sugar Harms: Ten Good Reasons for an Athlete to Avoid Simple Sugars

1. Sugar can suppress the immune system.

2. Sugar can cause difficulty with concentration and promote hyperactivity and anxiety.

3. Sugar can upset the mineral balance in the body.

4. Sugar can produce a rise in your triglycerides and a decrease in your good cholesterol.

5. Sugar can feed cancer growth.

6. Sugar contributes to the reduction in defenses against bacterial infections.

7. Too much sugar can lead to a chromium deficiency.

8 Sugar can increase fasting levels of glucose.

9. Sugar can cause hypoglycemia.

10. Sugar can produce an acidic digestive tract.

Fiber

Eating a lot of complex carbohydrates will automatically give you enough fiber. Fiber refers to the components of plant cell walls that are not digested by human intestinal enzymes. It is also called "roughage" or "bulk." When whole-grains are processed or refined, much of the fiber is removed and many of the nutrients are lost. Fiber adds bulk to the diet, absorbs water in the intestine and produces larger, softer stools that are easily eliminated. This decreases the time that cancer-causing agents are in contact with the lining of the large intestine and colon. This also inhibits the absorption of toxins into the bloodstream. People who consume a high-fiber diet have less colon cancer, heart disease, cholesterol problems, and gallstones. Soluble fiber forms a gel as it moves through the digestive system interfering with the absorption of cholesterol. Oat bran, oatmeal, barley, rice bran, apples, oranges, strawberries, prunes, carrots, corn, broccoli, lentils, navy beans and pinto beans all contain soluble fiber. Fiber of any kind is also great for weight loss and weight control as it fills the stomach and decreases appetite. Conditions associated with low-fiber diets are chronic constipation, diverticulitis, irritable bowel syndrome, Crohn's disease, colitis, and blood clots in veins and lungs. Cancer, heart disease, diabetes, and kidney problems have all been linked to low-fiber diets.

The optimal diet should have about 45 grams of fiber a day. Fruits, vegetables, legumes (beans), nuts, whole-grain breads, whole-grain cereals and brown rice are great choices. You can build up to this amount slowly so your digestive system will have time to adapt.

Protein

Protein's job is to build and repair body tissues, including muscles, tendons, and ligaments. It is also necessary for the synthesis of hormones, enzymes, and antibodies, as well as fluid transport and energy. In developed nations, especially the United States, it is very rare for insufficient protein intake to be a problem. Most of us eat too much, especially animal protein, and choose poor quality sources. Research suggests an active adult needs about 15% of their calories to be comprised of protein. Excess protein puts stress on the digestive tract, kidneys, and liver. Too much protein from animal sources causes an excess of uric acid in the bloodstream. Uric acid is a by-product of protein metabolism. In order to neutralize this acid, the body steals calcium from bones and other stores in the body, leaching the body of calcium. Some nutritionists and researchers believe the reason we need such a high intake of calcium is because of our extremely high intake of animal protein. Some even implicate the rise in osteoporosis with the increase in animal protein in our diets. The Nutrition Committee of the Council on Nutrition, Physical Activity, and Metabolism of the American Heart Association states, "High-protein diets are not recommended because they restrict healthful foods that provide essential nutrients and do not provide the variety of foods needed to adequately meet nutritional needs. Individuals who follow these diets are therefore at risk for compromised vitamin and mineral intake, as well as potential cardiac, renal, bone, and liver abnormalities overall."

Can athletes be vegetarians? Will they grow and perform just as well on plant foods? Yes. You can easily get the protein you need from fruits, vegetables, soy foods, beans, grains, seeds, and nuts. Research is showing that by keeping your animal food consumption to less than 10% of your total calories that you will help prevent disease as you get older. This means you don't have to be a complete vegetarian but you have to move in the direction of a "plant-based" diet to protect your health. Consume only protein supplements and energy bars made from plant protein such as soy-based smoothie mixes (see Recommended Resources). Research indicates that if you can keep your intake of animal foods to less than 10% of your caloric intake, your risk of disease goes down dramatically. This means you can get excellent protein from plant sources for many of your meals. Nuts, seeds, grains, beans, and soy products all contain high-quality protein. If you choose to eat beef and poultry choose organic, low-fat varieties and do not consume the skin. Free-range and grass-fed are best. Free-range eggs are a better choice as they have a higher ratio of omega-3 fatty acids. Purchase organic animal foods if you can, to reduce your consumption of steroids, antibiotics, growth hormone residues, etc. Think of animal food as a small condiment-sized serving instead of the main part of your plate.

Protein is not what builds muscle. Training is what builds muscle. Eating a balanced, 90% plant-based diet will give your body the building blocks it needs to do its thing. With the right choices, athletes can perform at a high level and still protect themselves from developing diseases in the future.

Fats

Fat is the primary fuel you use for light to moderate-intensity exercise. You should not consume more than 15% to 20% of your calories from fat. The essential fatty acids provided by the fat in your diet are important for maintaining healthy cell membranes, healthy skin, making hormones, and for transporting certain vitamins. The type of fat is the important thing. It is best to get your fat from food and not added oils.

Reduce Saturated Fat and Cholesterol

Animal food is the primary source for saturated fat in the diet. Fat on beef, pork, veal, the skin on poultry, dairy products like cheese, milk, lard, and butter, are all common sources of saturated fats. It is also found in palm oil, palm kernel oil, and coconut oil. There is overwhelming research showing that diets high in saturated fats raise the risk of heart disease, stroke, and many forms of cancer. One of the hardest foods to restrict is cheese. Cheese is very high in saturated fat and is included in almost everything we eat.

Avoid Trans-Fat or Hydrogenated Fat

These are fats that have been altered to make food products have a longer shelf life. They are very damaging and are mostly found in cookies, cakes, crackers, fast food, and other highly processed foods. Trans-fatty acids are very hard for your body to break down. They stick together causing fatty deposits in the arteries and the liver. Like saturated fat, they are associated with a higher incidence of heart disease and stroke and depress the immune system. If the label says a food has trans-fats—put it back. There are plenty of other choices without it.

The Good Fats

If you choose to consume oils, the best choices are monounsaturated fats like olive oil and canola oil. Good fats come from nuts, seeds, flax seeds, avocados, and olives. Remember that all oils are equally high in calories. It is best to get your fat calories from foods and not added oils. Carry a bag of raw almonds and walnuts mixed with dried fruit in your sports bag, add avocado and a few nuts to your salad, and put ground flaxseeds into your smoothie.

Omega-3 Fatty Acids

Every cell in our body needs omega-3 fatty acids to function optimally. We cannot manufacture them ourselves so they must be ingested. The omega-6 fatty acids are also essential but our modern diets contain plenty of this oil. During the last century people in developed countries like the United States have eliminated almost all omega-3 fatty acids from their diet. Where we used to have a ratio of one omega-6 to one omega-3, we now have a ratio of 20 omega-6s to one omega-3 in our diets.

What do omega-3 fatty acids do in the body? They help control energy production in the cell and they are the building blocks of your cell membranes, controlling what comes in and out of the cell. Research has discovered that this depletion of omega-3s has had a very negative effect on our bodies, particularly on the brain and the heart. The rise in heart disease and bi-polar depression has directly paralleled this decrease in omega-3 consumption. Other diseases related to this deficiency are rheumatoid arthritis, diabetes, postpartum depression, Crohn's disease, cancer, obesity, asthma, attention disorders, and aggression/hostility in teenagers.

There used to be an abundance of omega-3 fatty acids in the food supply especially in populations that ate fish and wild game. When cows and chickens were allowed to roam free and eat grass, the meat and eggs had a much higher content of omega-3s. Because our food supply has changed drastically people consume little or no omega-3s. Salmon that is farm-raised have no chance to eat the algae that makes wild, fatty fish high in this essential nutrient. Fish (certain species more than others) have also been contaminated with environmental pollutants like mercury and PCBs, which makes it less desirable to eat the amounts needed to get adequate omega-3s.

How to Get More Omega-3s:

Increase omega-3 fatty acids in your diet and decrease omega-6-containing oils (corn oil, safflower oil and sunflower oil).

Good sources of omega-3s are:

• Flax and hemp seeds (grind whole seeds in your coffee grinder).

• Walnuts.

• Soy foods/tofu.

• Oily fish (salmon, mackerel, tuna).

• Fortified eggs or eggs from free-range/grass-fed chickens.

• Wild game.

- High-quality/purified fish oil supplements although these are still risky because they can oxidize or spoil and can have contaminants. Many nutrition professionals no longer recommend consuming oil of any kind. (See Recommended Resources for more information and check with your registered dietitian or physician before consuming a supplement.)

What is Your pH? Acid versus Alkaline Diets

Research is showing that people who eat a more alkaline diet are healthier. Cancer cells and most diseases thrive in acidosis. Our body is able to heal itself if we provide a more alkaline environment. This means eating about 80% plant-based foods (fruits and vegetables) and about 20% acid foods (proteins like meat, fish, milk, eggs, and poultry as well as fats, grains, and sugars). This is the opposite of the typical American diet which focuses more on acidic foods. If you have eggs and bacon for breakfast, turkey and cheese for lunch and pasta and meatballs for dinner you are consuming a mostly acid diet.

Do Athletes Need Supplements? Whole Food versus Man-Made

Researchers are beginning to understand that vitamin supplements cannot make up for a poor diet and that isolated supplements rarely show any ability to prevent disease. In several studies, isolated, man-made supplements were found to cause more harm than good. If you think about this it makes sense. Our bodies need thousands of nutrients, so eating the whole food item works better than pulling out one nutrient and hoping that it will work by itself. We simply need to eat food in the way it was put on earth: whole and unprocessed.

> Everything is practice.
>
> —Pele, Brazilian Soccer Star

The government and researchers have spent billions of dollars and many decades trying to find a cure for heart disease, cancer and other diseases. They have tried to discover what is the one thing in the orange that is good for you. After years of study we now know that it is the synergy of the whole orange that allows your body to function at its very best. Food should be eaten in the proportion which it was put on earth, not in fragmented, isolated vitamins or man-made elements. There is overwhelming evidence that people who eat a variety of raw fruits, raw vegetables and unrefined grains have the least amount of disease. The problem is that very few humans actually consume the necessary amount and variety of these healthy foods. Sometimes a carefully chosen supplement can bridge the gap in your diet.

Guidelines for Choosing a Supplement:

This section is excerpted from *PowerPack for the Winning Edge* by Roy Vartabedian, PhD and Jack Medina, MA. See the Recommended Resources at the end of this book.

1. Are you sure the product does not contain any harmful or "extra" ingredients? Just because it is natural does not mean it is safe. Recently, popular children's vitamins were found to contain lead.

2. Does the supplement contain whole foods from real fruits, vegetables, and grains, or is it made of isolated, man-made vitamins?

3. Does it contain ingredients that have no proven benefit? Testimonials may be abundant, but there is no real, gold standard, peer-reviewed, published research showing that the supplement is actually absorbed and has benefits in the body.

4. Was the research done on the actual product and not a selected generic ingredient? Does the research show benefits in the human body (not rats)? Is there a placebo group (where one group gets the real thing and the other gets a sugar pill)? Is it a double-blind study, in which nobody knows who got the product and who got the placebo, until the study is over? Is it published in a

peer-reviewed scientific journal (real and independent science)?

5. Does the company that makes the supplement make fantastic or unbelievable claims about their product? Do they use famous people or professional athletes with testimonials? Words like "miracle," "cure," "amazing," "secret formula," and testimonials about diseases that were cured should raise red flags. Only prescription drugs may claim to treat or cure diseases, not supplements.

Whole Food Supplements

People know they should eat more fruits and vegetables but in reality it is not happening. If you know you do not eat 9 to 13 fruits and vegetables each day, the best insurance is a whole food supplement. This is especially important in athletes because of the extra oxidative stress and free radical damage from training so hard. I recommend one to my clients called Juice Plus+®. Taking Juice Plus+® capsules every day provides the nutritional foundation we so desperately need and that is so lacking in our diets today. Juice Plus+® is not a vitamin supplement providing a limited number of handpicked nutrients. Juice Plus+® is a whole-food based product providing the wide array of nutrients found in a variety of nutritious fruits, vegetables, and grains. It's the next best thing to fruits and vegetables because we don't get nearly enough of the real thing every day. Juice Plus+® comes in capsules, chewables, and gummies. It is certified as gluten-free and is kosher. This is one of the very few supplements that I recommend because it has a large body of primary, peer-reviewed research to show that it improves immune function, improves circulation, lowers inflammation, and reduces oxidative stress in normal people and in athletes. Juice Plus+® has been analyzed to determine what's in it, where it goes in the body, and what it does when it gets there. This is very rare in the supplement world. Juice Plus+® is the perfect answer for those of us who try hard in our busy lives but don't always get the recommended 9 to 13 fruits and veggies into our systems every day. See the Recommended Resources for ordering information.

Protecting the Athlete's Bones

Bones are living tissues, constantly being remodeled and reacting to hormonal changes, nutrition, and stressors applied to them. Osteoporosis is a disease in which low bone mass and deterioration of bone structure causes bones to be weak, porous, brittle, and susceptible to fracture. At highest risk are Asian and Caucasian females who are relatively thin and sedentary, postmenopausal women without estrogen support, and those with a family history of osteoporosis. Black females are at lower risk possibly because of greater bone mass. Men can develop osteoporosis but it usually shows up much later in life.

Researchers are beginning to realize that the main cause of osteoporosis is a high intake of acidic food, mainly animal protein. The higher the intake of protein, the more uric acid is produced which must be neutralized by calcium from bones and teeth. Animal products and processed foods contain high levels of phosphorous, which also has to be neutralized with calcium. Osteoporosis is linked with kidney disorders because of the high stress on the kidneys to eliminate the leftovers from protein metabolism. The answer is to eat a diet high in fruits and vegetables, which have a high calcium-to-phosphorous ratio. Plant-based calcium is much more available and easy to absorb and it prevents the leaching out of calcium from bones and teeth. Try to increase tofu, soy products (processed with calcium sulphate or calcium chloride), raw almonds, calcium-fortified orange juice, bok choy, broccoli, kale, turnip greens, parsley, mustard greens, and endive. Calcium is not effective without vitamin D, so consume foods fortified with added vitamin D like orange juice, soy milk, and cereals. Other foods with vitamin D include egg yolks, salmon, and sardines. Exposure to sunshine for 10 to 15 minutes without sunscreen allows your body to make its own vitamin D. Never stay out long enough to burn.

What About Dairy Foods?

The only drink that is biologically necessary after weaning is water. Recent research is finding that dairy products may not be the health food that we once thought they were. For one thing, the pasteurized, homogenized milk that we drink is very different than the raw form people drank in the past. Dairy foods are a huge source of saturated fat. Whole milk is 49% fat and even 2% milk derives 35% of its calories from fat. Most cheeses are about 70% fat. Saturated fat is linked to insulin resistance, higher cholesterol, heart disease, and stroke. Dairy sugar is called lactose. About 55% of the calories in fat-free milk actually come from this sugar. Many people are lactose intolerant, which can cause severe stomach upset. The protein in dairy foods has come under scrutiny for contributing to type 1 diabetes, loss of kidney function in diabetics, prostate cancer, and ovarian cancer. Migraine sufferers and people with rheumatoid arthritis may find that dairy protein is a trigger for attacks. Cows' milk is high in phosphorous, which can combine with calcium and can prevent you from absorbing the calcium in milk. Milk protein also accelerates calcium excretion from the blood through the kidneys. This is also true when you eat large amounts of meat and poultry products. Vegans (vegetarians who do not consume dairy or eggs) will need about 50% less calcium than meat eaters because they lose much less calcium in their urine. If you consume less animal protein in general you will actually need less calcium because your diet is more alkaline than acid. Most people consume dairy for the calcium but it is very easy to get calcium from plant foods. You would be surprised how great organic soy milk, rice milk, and almond milk taste. Most of these come in vanilla, chocolate, and strawberry flavors. Look for products that are not genetically modified. They will be labeled as non-GM.

Avoid These to Prevent Osteoporosis:

- Tobacco—Lowers hormone levels, thereby accelerating bone loss. Stopping smoking at any age slows bone loss. Stay away from second-hand smoke as well.

- High caffeine intake—Increases the amount of calcium excreted in the urine, depriving the bones of calcium they need. Carbonated sodas have phosphates, which cause loss of calcium from bones and teeth.

- Alcohol consumption—Suppresses bone tissue formation.

- Excessive dieting—Hurts the bones by depriving the body of important nutrients, including calcium. Eating disorders can also affect bone health.

- Excessive physical activity—Can cause bone loss by depressing hormone levels, evident when a female athlete begins to miss her normal menstrual periods (amenorrhea).

Strategies for Preventing Osteoporosis

- Consume a calcium-rich diet—calcium is essential to healthy bones. This is extremely important during the teen years and early adulthood when we build our peak bone density, but also throughout our lives. Vegetable sources are best, including almonds, calcium-fortified juice, tofu, soy products (processed with calcium sulphate or calcium chloride), bok choy, broccoli, kale, turnip greens, canned sardines, salmon with bones, Juice Plus+ Complete® smoothie, or calcium supplements as needed. It is best to get your calcium from food sources.

- Vitamin D—Necessary for our bodies to absorb calcium. Good sources are sunshine, fortified foods like orange juice, soy milk, rice milk, and cereals. Also include salmon, sardines, egg yolks, and Toni's Smoothie (recipe in What to Eat Chapter).

- Weight Bearing Exercise—Running or jogging and soccer are perfect. Most sports involve weight-bearing exercise, except swimming and cycling. Just be sure to add some strength training for the arms and upper body. Research shows this is very important for maintaining bone health.

- Consult a physician or registered dietitian—learn about your risk for osteoporosis and the recommended treatment.

Athletes need to ingest sufficient energy to meet the physical demands of their intense and oftentimes lengthy training sessions. Consuming the right amounts and types of food and fluid will provide their body with the fuel needed to achieve optimal training benefits and peak performance.

—Tina Marie Mendieta MS, RD/LDN

The Winning Goal

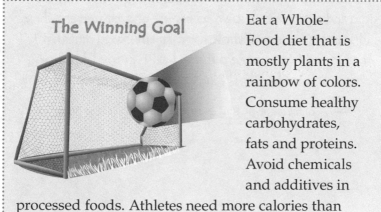

Eat a Whole-Food diet that is mostly plants in a rainbow of colors. Consume healthy carbohydrates, fats and proteins. Avoid chemicals and additives in processed foods. Athletes need more calories than non-athletes but they should still be healthy calories.

These findings show that heart disease, diabetes, and obesity can be reversed by a healthy diet. Other research shows that various cancers, autoimmune diseases, bone health, kidney health, vision and brain disorders in old age (like cognitive dysfunction and Alzheimer's) are convincingly influenced by diet. Most importantly, the diet that has time and again been shown to reverse and/or prevent these diseases is the same whole foods, plant-based diet that I had found to promote optimal health in my laboratory research and in the China Study. The findings are consistent.

—T. Colin Campbell, PhD excerpted from *The China Study*

11. Eating In, Eating Out, and Grocery Shopping: A Practical Guide for Athletes

What to Eat Before, During and After Soccer Practice and Games

Carbohydrates like cereal, pasta, bread, rice, vegetables, and fruits are the main fuel for training and competition. Glycogen in the liver and in muscles needs to be replaced by carbohydrates in the diet. Failure to recover glycogen stores leads to early fatigue, lower exercise intensity, and increased risk for illness and injury.

What to eat before practice

What you eat the three days before is more important than the night before. Eating healthy all the time is the best strategy. A diet that is only 50% carbohydrate will eventually lead to a decline of glycogen in your muscles and liver. An athlete's diet should be at least 60% to 70% carbohydrate to maintain energy stores. The closer you eat to the time of heavy activity, the smaller the meal should be. A heavy meal could lead to cramping and low energy. Your muscles are competing with your digestive system for blood flow and energy. Good pre-game choices include fruit, vegetables, pasta, baked potato, healthy snack bars, whole grain toast or

English muffins with spreadable fruit. Poor choices include animal protein and high-fat foods such as chicken nuggets and fries or a steak dinner, that are slower to digest, can cause cramping, and can make you sluggish during your activity.

What to eat after practice or after the game

Within 30 minutes of a hard training session (or as soon as possible) consume a meal or snack containing about 80% carbohydrate and 20% protein. A peanut/almond butter and fruit spread sandwich, raw almonds and dried fruit, beans and rice, pasta and veggies, or a fruit and plant protein smoothie (recipe on page 126) would be great.

What to eat during a competition or a long tournament

Drink water between each game or activity session and take small bites to keep your energy up. Orange, kiwi, or apple slices, a banana, a couple of raisins, plain bread or a bagel would all work. Do not consume anything with a high fat or protein content or a drink with a high sugar content.

Meal and Snack Ideas for Soccer Athletes in Training

- Cereal (whole-grain with soy or rice milk) with fruit.

- Whole grain sandwich with hummus, spreadable fruit and peanut/almond butter, veggies, organic turkey.

- Brown or wild rice with veggies or beans.

- Whole grain tortilla wrap with veggies, beans, salsa, and avocados.

- Pita pocket with veggies, tuna, salmon, or hummus.

- Whole grain pasta with veggies and/or tomato sauce.

- Fruit of any kind (bananas and kiwi are great, fresh pineapple has an enzyme that repairs muscle).

- Baked potato or sweet potato.

- Oatmeal.

- Raw almonds, pecans, or walnuts mixed with dried fruit.

- Parfait with fruit and granola.

- Celery and peanut/almond butter.

- Raw veggies with hummus or a low-fat dip.

- Baked tortilla chips with salsa.

- Graham crackers or gingersnaps dipped in applesauce.

- Mini rice cakes with peanut/almond butter.

- Healthy sports bars/granola bars are preferable to fast food or vending machines (try Kashi® brand or a bar with low sugar, high-fiber, and a plant-based protein source).

- Homemade banana bread, corn bread, or muffins.

• Juice Plus+ Complete® smoothie with fruit (recipe below).

Healthy Recipes

Toni's Smoothie Recipe for Athletes (and Tired Parents)

This can be altered to fit your taste buds. It is a complete meal replacement, quick and healthy breakfast or after-training snack to reload muscle glycogen. This provides over half of your day's worth of calcium—all from plant sources. I have found that a good blender makes all the difference. My kids like it to be smooth! (*Hint:* For extra creamy smoothies, peel ripe bananas and freeze them ahead of time.) Play around with it until you find a combination that you love.

French Vanilla Smoothie with Fruit
Blend until smooth
>   *1 cup of vanilla soy milk, plain soy milk, almond milk,*
>   *rice milk, water, or calcium fortified juice*
>   *1 scoop of French Vanilla Juice Plus+ Complete® (see*
>   *Recommended Resources to order)*
>   *1 ripe banana*
>   *1 Tablespoon brewer's yeast or nutritional yeast*
>   *(provides B vitamins, an important addition for*
>   *vegetarians)*
>   *1 Tablespoon ground flax seed for Omega 3s (just put*
>   *whole seeds in a small coffee grinder)*

Frozen or fresh fruit
I like to use a few strawberries, peaches, raspberries,
      blackberries, and blueberries
Ice (optional but makes it thicker and colder)

Chocolate Banana Smoothie
Blend until smooth
   1 cup of vanilla soy milk, plain soy milk, rice milk,
      almond milk, or water
   1 scoop of Dutch Chocolate Juice Plus+ Complete®
      (see Recommended Resources to order)
   1 ripe banana
   1 Tablespoon brewer's yeast or nutritional yeast
   1 Tablespoon ground flaxseed for Omega 3s (just put
      whole seeds in a small coffee grinder)
   1 cup of ice

Jenna's Favorite Parfait

Start with a pretty, long-stemmed glass and layer the following
ingredients. You can make it the night before if you prefer
granola that is not too crunchy. Top it with a whole strawberry
or a design of berries. Pick a pattern and then repeat.
   Strawberries, blueberries, blackberries, or pineapple
      (any fresh or thawed frozen fruit will work)
   Granola (organic if possible)
   Organic yogurt or non-dairy yogurt
   Dried dates or raisins

Wrap-Ups to Go

This is a great way to get several veggies in at once. Easy to pack and carry. Put it next to a cold or frozen water bottle to keep it cool for several hours.

Whole wheat tortillas or flatbread
Filling: choice of hummus, black or kidney beans, organic
*   turkey, wild salmon, or other healthy choice*
Shredded carrots, purple cabbage, cucumbers, spinach,
*   sprouts, red peppers, corn or any other veggies*
Healthy salad dressing (optional)

Sports Bag Trail Mix

(Place in a small zip-lock snack bag—make enough for the whole week)

5 or 6 raw almonds
5 or 6 raw walnuts
3 Brazil nuts
¼ cup dried apricots
¼ cup dried plums
Pieces of healthy cereal or granola (about 8 pieces)

Tips for Eating Out and Choosing Wisely

- Choose foods that are broiled instead of fried, such as a grilled chicken sandwich instead of fried chicken or chicken nuggets, grilled fish instead of fried fish, etc.

- Choose soups that are broth or tomato-based and not cream based.

- Choose a tomato-based or broth-based sauce instead of Alfredo or cream sauce for pasta. If they have whole wheat pasta, ask for this as a substitute.

- Always ask for your salad dressing on the side. Have low-fat salad dressings instead of the full-fat kind. Romaine, leaf lettuce or spinach are much more nutritious than iceberg lettuce.

- Always substitute another side dish for French fries. Most restaurants will bring you broccoli or the veggie of the day. Some offer fruit or a salad as a choice. Baked potatoes or sweet potatoes without the butter or sour cream (or with a tiny amount) are better than fries.

- Use mustard or ketchup instead of mayonnaise.

- When ordering a sub or sandwich, select the veggie choice or leaner meats like turkey or grilled chicken. Stay away from fried items like burgers or steak and cheese sandwiches.

- Choose water instead of sodas, fruit drinks, and milkshakes.

- When ordering pizza, add lots of veggies instead of meat. Ask for half the cheese or no cheese.

- When ordering Chinese or Asian food, ask for no MSG (this is a chemical preservative and taste enhancer) and ask that veggies be steamed with the sauce on the side to decrease the fat. Avoid fried foods. Ask for brown rice if available.

- If fruit and veggies are available, try to add them into your meal. For example, have lettuce and tomato on sandwiches or burgers.

Some Ideas for Popular Restaurants

Burger King®, Fuddruckers®, and Backyard Burger®, as well as other restaurants offer a veggie burger. You owe it to yourself to be brave and try it with lettuce, tomato, onion, ketchup and mustard.

At our local Mexican restaurant I have them make a naked burrito in a bowl with cilantro rice, black beans, and pinto beans. Heap on the chunky salsa and lots of lettuce. This is a delicious vegetarian meal with plenty of plant-based protein. Yes, you have to leave off the cheese!

At Italian restaurants, (Macaroni Grill® and Nothing but Noodles® are the ones we have) I order whole wheat pasta with tomato-basil sauce. I add broccoli, carrots, sun dried tomatoes and mushrooms. Delicious! Some of my best meals have been when I ask the waiter for a plate of their best vegetables. The chefs seem to really like this and they send a beautiful plate every time!

A broth or tomato-based soup with bread is always a good choice.

Almost every restaurant has a grilled or blackened salmon choice. Ask for vegetables and a baked potato to eat with it.

If You Have to Eat Fast Food

You can check out your favorite fast food place or restaurant on the Internet. You can find the company Web site by doing a Google search. Once you have found the Web site, look for the "nutrition section." There is usually a link on the home page to the nutrition section where you will find nutrition facts, including fat, cholesterol, sodium, protein, calories, and more. This will help you make better choices when eating out. Here are a few examples of poor choices and somewhat better choices when you have to eat fast food. You will see that most of the "better" choices have huge amounts of sodium and very few nutrients. Look for mostly vegetable salads, fruit, baked potatoes, or veggie burgers at many restaurants. Try to limit fast food to once a week at the most. Check for trans-fat (especially in chicken nuggets) and avoid all of these foods. For instance some restaurants have stopped using trans-fat but others continue to use it.

McDonalds® Poor Choices

Small Fries (250 calories; 13 grams fat; 140 mg sodium)
Large Fries (570 calories; 30 grams fat; 330 mg sodium)
Quarter Pounder with Cheese (510 calories; 26 grams fat; 1190 mg sodium)
Nuggets 6 Pack (250 calories; 15 grams fat; 670 mg sodium)
Strawberry Triple-Thick Shake (1110 calories; 27 grams fat; 130 mg sodium)

McDonalds® Better Choices

Fruit and Yogurt Parfait (180 calories; 2 grams fat; 85 mg sodium)
Southwest Salad with Grilled Chicken (320 calories; 9 grams fat; 970 mg sodium)

Chic-fil-A® Poor Choices

Chicken Biscuit (420 calories; 19 grams fat; 1270 mg sodium)
Chicken Sandwich (410 calories; 16 grams fat; 1300 mg sodium)

Better Choices at Chic-fil-A®

Char-grilled Sandwich (ask for lettuce and tomato; 270 calories; 3.5 grams fat; 940 mg sodium)
Char-grilled Salad (This is without dressing/choose low fat or non-fat; 180 calories; 6 grams fat; 620 mg sodium)
Fruit Bowl (50 calories; 0 grams fat; 0 mg sodium)

Side Salad (60 calories; 3 grams fat; 75 mg sodium)
Hearty Breast of Chicken Soup (140 calories; 3.5 grams fat;
    900 mg sodium)

Taco Bell® Poor Choices

Grilled Beef Burrito (680 calories; 30 grams fat; 2120 mg sodium)
Fiesta Taco Salad (840 calories; 45 grams fat; 1780 mg sodium)
    (without shell 470 calories; 25 grams fat; 1510 mg sodium)

Taco Bell® Better Choices

Crunchy Tacos (150 calories; 8 grams fat; 370 mg sodium)
Grilled Steak Soft Shell (160 calories; 4.5 grams fat; 550 mg sodium)
Spicy Chicken Soft Taco (170 calories; 6 grams fat; 580 mg sodium)

Wendy's® Poor Choices

Big Bacon Classic Sandwich (590 calories; 30 grams fat;
    1510 mg sodium)
Chicken Club Sandwich (650 calories; 31 grams fat; 1580 mg sodium)
Medium Chocolate Frosty (430 calories; 55 grams sugar)

Wendy's® Better Choices

Sour Cream and Chives Baked Potato (320 calories; 4 grams fat;
    55 mg sodium)
Mandarin Chicken Salad (170 calories; 2 grams fat; 480 mg
    sodium; add dressing: 190 calories)
Caesar Chicken Salad (90 calories; 5 grams fat; 620 mg sodium;
    add dressing: 120 calories)

Burger King® Poor Choices

*Double Whopper w/cheese (990 calories; 64 grams fat;
1520 mg sodium)*

*Spicy Chicken Sandwich (720 calories; 36 grams fat;
2000 mg sodium)*

Onion Rings—Large (450 calories; 22 grams fat; 660 mg sodium)

Burger King® Better Choices

*Chicken Garden Salad (240 calories; 9 grams fat; 720 mg
sodium; add light Italian dressing: 120 calories; 11 grams
fat; 440 mg sodium)*

*Chicken Tenders—5 pc. (210 calories; 12 grams fat; 600 mg
sodium)*

*BK Veggie Burger (without the mayo or the cheese; 340 calories;
8 grams fat; 1030 mg sodium)*

Grocery Shopping—Be a Smart Consumer

- Try to buy foods that contain ingredients you recognize or would use at home.

- Stay on the perimeter of the grocery store. This is where the fresh, whole food is sold.

- Avoid products containing the following ingredients: trans fats, partially hydrogenated oils, artificial sweeteners (aspartame or Splenda®), MSG, nitrites, nitrates, artificial colors, sulfites, potassium bromate, and brominated vegetable oil.

• The following terms all mean one thing—sugar! Brown sugar, honey, dextrose, maltose, lactose, fructose, rock sugar, and corn syrup and high-fructose corn syrup—these are all terms for the same thing. No one sugar is healthier or better than another, they are all simply empty calories and replace healthier choices. High sugar in your diet will depress your immune system and compromise your health.

• Check serving sizes. Most of us eat much more than a typical serving. A small bag of chips might actually be 2½ servings. This is a sneaky trick! You must multiply the calories and fat by the number of servings in the package, or by 2.5 in this case, to get your total nutritional intake.

What is a serving size?

It is more important to eat a variety of fruits and vegetables of many colors than to worry about the exact serving size. Most foods are ½ cup per serving. Loose foods like lettuce are one cup and dried fruit and nuts (denser foods) are ¼ cup. Athletes often need more calories than less active people but the extra servings should still come from healthy sources.

Foods That Drain the Body and Brain

White bread, white sugar, alcohol, artificial sweeteners, artificial food colorings, colas, frostings, corn syrup, nitrate and nitrate-containing foods, hot dogs, cured meats, high sugar drinks, candy, nicotine, processed snacks, fast food with high fat and sodium, and any foods with a long list of ingredients you don't recognize as real foods.

Super Foods for Serious Athletes— Choose Some to Eat Every Day

Nutrition-packed food choices that will improve your performance and help to prevent illness now and when you are older! Research is showing that these foods truly can make a difference:

Wild salmon, beans, walnuts, avocados, brazil nuts, spinach, blueberries, sweet potatoes, broccoli, cinnamon, garlic, collard greens, kale, brown rice, bananas, kiwi, soy, oranges, onions, dried fruit—apricots, figs, plums, raisins, dates, cranberries—tomatoes, black and green tea, and pumpkin.

Before games our team always eats together at someone's house. This gives us a chance to prepare for the game together and have a home cooked dinner instead of a fast food pre-game meal.

Rob M., Varsity Soccer Player, Age 17, Charlotte Latin School

The Winning Goal

Eating well takes planning and self-control. What you eat day after day is more important to your performance than what you eat right before you compete. Enlist your entire family so you can make healthy changes together. Be a role model for good nutrition on your team.

The vision of a champion is someone who is
bent over, drenched in sweat, at the point of
exhaustion when nobody else is watching.

—Anson Dorance, Head Soccer Coach, UNC Chapel Hill

12. Hydration for Soccer Players

Everyone, including athletes, should drink at least 6 to 8 glasses (8-ounces) of water each day or half their weight in ounces. Children should consume half of their weight in ounces. A 50-lb child would need 25 ounces per day. Adequate fluid intake is necessary to replace fluids lost through metabolism, daily activity, soccer, and other vigorous exercise. The amount lost depends on many factors including environmental temperature, humidity, and your ability to dissipate heat. When you are dehydrated, even just a little, studies have shown your energy level will drop as well as your ability to focus. Every system in your body depends on water to work properly. Cooler water is absorbed faster than warm or room temperature fluids. Drink water before, during, and after your practice. Foods like bananas, pineapples, oranges, and kiwis will help maintain the electrolytes that you need for long workouts. Sports drinks with a high sugar content can cause cramping and are not recommended. A drink like Propel®, with a tiny bit of carbohydrate, may improve taste and help athletes consume more fluid. You can also add lemons, limes, or a little cranberry or grape juice to water to improve the taste. For extreme endurance events, drinks containing electrolytes and carbohydrate are sometimes needed but for a normal practice or game, water is usually the best choice. It is important to consume water that has the minerals intact or you will pull calcium and minerals from your body to balance the blood levels. Filtered water from a carbon filter will leave the minerals intact, a reverse-osmosis filter will remove the minerals. Distilled water is not a good choice for drinking for this reason.

> I want my team to be acclimated to the heat
> BEFORE the season starts. They have to learn
> to pre-hydrate and make it a habit.
>
> —Lee Horton, Coach, Charlotte Latin School, Charlotte Lady
> Eagles, Player, UNC Chapel Hill, North Carolina Soccer Hall
> of Fame Inductee, South Charlotte Soccer Association

Guidelines for Exercise Fluid Replacement

- Consume 8 to 16 ounces of fluid at least one hour before the start of practice or the game.

- Consume 4 to 8 ounces of fluid every 10 to 15 minutes during the workout.

- Consume 16 to 24 ounces during the 30 minutes after exercise even if you do not feel thirsty.

- For serious athletes it is a good idea to weigh yourself before and after practice to monitor your fluid loss.

What's the Big Deal About Soft Drinks?

Athletes (and their families) have no reason to consume regular or diet sodas. They can only hurt performance and decrease health. At most, sodas should be an occasional treat. There are many reasons to avoid soft drinks:

• They have a high sugar content (23 grams for 8 ounces, which is about 6 teaspoons for every 8 ounces).

• They contain no nutrients (we call this "empty or liquid calories").

• They are high in phosphorous, which depletes calcium from bones and teeth.

• They replace healthy choices like water.

• Diet drinks have aspartame and Splenda® (chemicals).

• Many contain caffeine (addictive, depletes bones).

Ten Ways to Add More Water to Your Day

1. Pre-hydrate! Always carry a bottle of water with you in the car. Drink on the way to your destination and on the way home.

2. Ice it down! Cold water tastes better.

3. Set a goal. For adults, fill two 32-ounce containers in the morning and make it a goal to finish them before bedtime. Young athletes should drink half their weight in ounces of water.

4. Ask your teachers if you can keep a bottle of water on your desk at school to sip all day. Your brain is 85% water and cannot function or focus without proper hydration.

5. Drink with a straw. It goes down faster and easier.

6. Squeeze in lemon, lime, or orange juice to add a bit of flavor.

7. Humans sometimes mistake thirst for hunger. When you are hungry start with a glass of water.

8. Eat fruits and vegetables that contain a lot of water, such as watermelon, oranges, celery, carrots, and lettuce.

9. Next time you start to order a soda stop and get water with lemon. You have just saved yourself ten teaspoons of sugar or more. Your body will thank you.

10. Be a role model at practice and at games. Make sure all the other kids seeing you drink water instead of sodas or sugary drinks.

Many popular sports drinks are high in sugar and lack many nutrients, making them essentially empty calories. The body does not hydrate efficiently with substances other than water, which should be the first-choice beverage for an athlete. Electrolytes, which are found in many sports drinks, are easily obtained with the proper diet.

—Pamela A. Popper, PhD, ND
From *The Wellness Forum's Guide to Sports Nutrition*

The Winning Goal

Water is necessary for every function in your body. Humans have a faulty thirst mechanism so you have to take purposeful water breaks and make a plan to stay hydrated before, during, and after training or a competition.

I am happy that the young girls have a lot more choices these days and an opportunity to feel better about themselves. If this encourages one girl to go out there, and not necessarily try soccer, but just do something she was nervous about doing or achieve something that she wasn't sure she could do, it's a wonderful feeling. Whether it's stopping to say hello or signing an autograph or scoring a memorable goal for them. It's worth it.

—Mia Hamm on being a role model and soccer icon

13. Body Image and Disordered Eating

—with Charee Boulter, PhD, Psychologist

It wasn't until I lost a match to someone ranked 200 places below me that I realized that I had no more energy left. I turned on the television one day, and there was a show on about eating disorders. I saw myself in the people on the show and decided it was time to do something about my eating disorder and the stress that was dominating my life.

—Zina Garrison, tennis player and two-time Olympic medalist, Federated Cup Captain

Although Zina is a female athlete, eating disorders are also becoming increasingly more prevalent in males. Guys, please read this chapter—you may help save a life.

Adolescence is a time when many changes are happening to your body. As you mature your body begins to transform from the body of child to a more adult body. During this time questions about your appearance are common. There is considerable pressure to have the "right look" that is promoted in magazines, on TV and in the movies.

For an athlete, the awareness of physical changes in appearance and in the body's ability to adapt to these changes can be heightened. Soccer maneuvers that once were easy may be more difficult during a growth spurt. Because athletes have more muscle, you might weigh more than your friends who are the same size. On the other hand you may find that you are thinner than your athletic peers and worry that you are not strong enough. As a soccer player you may find that your awareness of these physical changes is amplified, because you spend several hours per week training with your teammates.

Athletes are at increased risk of developing concerns about their body image and, therefore, eating disorders. Coaches and others may mistakenly assume that lower body fat is positively related to increased performance. Popular sports magazines commonly have weight loss articles. A player who over-trains may be rewarded for his/her dedication. Increased public awareness of the use of "performance enhancing" drugs and supplements (some illegal) by professional athletes, has sent messages about the lengths some individuals will go to in their attempt to win. Gaining an edge over one's competition through healthy or unhealthy means can be tempting for amateur athletes.

Individual feelings of self-doubt and self-consciousness can lead an athlete to criticize his or her body. Comments from your coach on body position, which are intended to help you improve your form and skills, can sound harsh and critical. On a day when you are feeling low, comments such as "use your strength, run faster," may sound like criticisms of your body. Thus, such a statement may be interpreted as "my legs are too short" or "my legs are too soft and weak."

If you are concerned that you or a friend may be struggling with body image concerns what should you do? How do you know if it is a body image issue or the common self-doubts of adolescence? Check the lists below to help you determine if it is a body image issue and what to do.

Signs of body image dissatisfaction

• Frequently makes negative comments about one's self.

• Avoids shopping for clothes with others (especially trying on clothes in common dressing rooms).

• Frequently asks about one's appearance—"Does this look OK?"

• Has frequent "bad hair" days.

• Moods are connected to feelings about appearance and/or weight.

• Makes comments about the appearance of others—both positive and negative.

- Compares self to others—"She is so pretty and I'm not. Her life is perfect." "He is so strong and ripped. He never sits on the bench."

- Thoughts and worries about appearance interfere with daily activities.

- It is difficult to concentrate and stay focused during practice or competition.

- Getting dressed takes too long due to multiple clothing changes.

What to say to a friend struggling with body image issues

- Make positive comments about his/her personality and talents.

- If she makes negative self-comments, tell her that you feel sad when she says such things about herself.

- Reassure her that she is beautiful inside and out.

- Avoid making comments about your own physical appearance and others'.

- Make an effort to focus on the strengths and functions of the body rather than the appearance of one's body.

Sometimes when an athlete struggles with body image concerns he/she may begin to diet and/or use supplements in an attempt to change his/her body shape. It is important to remember that healthy nutrition is key to optimal functioning. Diets often eliminate crucial nutrients and/or adequate calories, placing an athlete at risk for a variety of physical problems, e.g. exhaustion, weakness, stress fractures, etc. Weight loss or muscle-building supplements can contain harmful ingredients. When diets go awry, disordered eating can be the result.

An eating disorder is complex and is much more than a body image disturbance combined with an out-of-control diet. There are many factors related to the development of an eating disorder. An athlete is not "crazy" if he or she develops an eating disorder. In fact some of the personal attributes that help an athlete excel can also place him at risk of developing an eating disorder; such as, being high achieving, goal-directed, and paying attention to detail. Some players may appear confident but may actually struggle with low self-esteem. Some may have a family history of eating disorders or other mental health disorders that place them at increased risk.

An eating disorder can have significant negative effects on one's health. The most serious is death. In 1994, Christy Henrich, a gymnast, died due to health complications related to an eating disorder. Problems that may be of heightened concern for athletes include:

- Fatigue.

- Dizziness.

- Decreased ability to concentrate.

- Increased overuse injuries.

- Stress fractures.

- Decreased cardiac functioning (increased risk of heart failure).

- Weakened immune system.

- Osteopenia or osteoporosis.

It is important to know the common signs of an eating disorder. If you recognize these signs in yourself or a friend, please talk to a trusted adult and seek professional assistance:

- Noticeable weight changes in a short period of time.

- Excessive dieting, even after achieving original goal.

- Belief that one is fat even though he/she is not.

- Belief that one is too skinny or weak even though he/she is not.

- Changes in eating patterns, such as eating alone, eating limited types of food.

- Avoiding social events where food is served.

- Uncontrolled binge eating.

- Use of dieting, purging, exercise or medications to compensate for overeating.

- Use of diet pills, weight loss or weight gain supplements, steroids, etc.

- Mood is dependent upon weight.

- Loss of menstrual period.

> My eating habits were a mess. For six or seven years, I was bulimic. A lot of that was my attitude that I would do anything to win—it was no one's fault but mine—my perfectionism, my need to win.
>
> —Megan Neyer—Eight-Time NCAA Champion Diver

Help is available for players struggling with disordered eating. Comprehensive treatment usually involves medical care, individual and group therapy, and nutritional therapy. A treatment team, which may include a physician, a therapist, and a dietitian, is often developed to address the athlete holistically. In some cases the coach may be included in some aspects of this treatment team, for example if the athlete needs to take some time away from training during recovery. Family therapy is often a component of treatment. In most cases outpatient treatment is sufficient. Some individuals may need more intensive care and thus may spend time in a residential treatment center or an inpatient hospital.

If you suspect that a friend is struggling with an eating disorder express your concerns to her/him. She/he may be embarrassed and try to hide the disorder, so do not worry if she does not seem happy that you are expressing your concern.

- Find a time when you are not likely to be interrupted.
- Use "I" messages to identify your concern and avoid accusing your friend of having a problem. "I am worried about you."
- Identify specific concerns such as: noticeable changes in eating patterns, physical fatigue, negative body image, etc.
- "I have noticed you seem really tired and you have been dieting a lot. I am concerned that you might have an eating disorder."
- Be a good listener.
- She/he might open up and share her struggles with you.
- He/she might deny having a problem.
- You can be a good friend and listen.
- Be understanding.

- Remember that having an eating disorder does not make a person crazy.

- You can probably relate to some of his/her feelings and concerns, but to a lesser degree.

- Ask your friend to see a professional—a doctor, a counselor or a nutritionist.

Treatment for an eating disorder can be lengthy. Sometimes an athlete may begin to make improvements by addressing the underlying issues—family issues, depressed mood, low self esteem—before the eating behaviors improve. Be patient. The end result of successful treatment is worth it.

The Winning Goal

You cannot fix eating disorders yourself. Get professional help or recommend help for your friend.

If you are not getting playing time reach deep for more determination. Hard work and extra practice will help you overcome your weaknesses. There is always someone out there working harder than you. Even if you are good you can always be better.

—Will L. , Age 17, Student, Basketball Player

14. Getting the Most Out of Summer Camps and Outside Training Programs

$\int$ummer camps and intensive sport programs are excellent ways to improve your skills, become more versatile, and learn from great coaches and former athletes. This is a chance to build your skills without the stress of competition. You may get more "game time" at a camp than you do during your season on your regular team. You may attend these programs with your team or a group of friends or you may sign up and go as an individual. Some are on weekends and some are entire weeks during the summer or holiday vacations. Some summer camps require a personal invitation either by a recommendation from your coach, by trying out in person or by sending in a video of yourself. If your goal is to compete at the high school, collegiate, or professional level, special camps are a great way to buff up your skills and be seen by the people that matter.

How to pack for a camp

Food and Drinks

• Water bottle or cooler of drinks (sometimes you have only a few seconds for water breaks so don't waste them waiting in line at the water fountain or the water table).

Lots of "10-second snacks"

• Baggies of whole grain cereal with dried fruit.

• Fruit of any kind—orange slices, apples—remember fresh pineapple has an enzyme that repairs muscle.

• Raw almonds and walnuts mixed with dried fruit.

• Healthy sports bars/granola bars are preferable to fast food or vending machines (try Kashi® brand or a bar with low sugar, high-fiber, and a plant-based protein source).

• Homemade banana bread or muffins.

• Whole grain bagel with peanut/almond butter.

Ideas for packing lunch for camp

• Sandwich with hummus, spreadable fruit and peanut/almond butter, organic turkey.

• Tortilla wrap with veggies, beans and avocados.

• Pita pocket with veggies, tuna, hummus, etc.

• Fruit, bananas, cut up kiwi, orange slices, or fresh pineapple.

Other Things You'll Want to Remember

• First aid items such as band-aids, toe tape, ankle or knee brace if you use one.

• Toiletries and hair supplies: deodorant, hairbrush, hairspray, ponytail holders, barrettes.

• An extra pair of shoes—or at least laces in case one breaks.

• Socks—switch to dry socks halfway through each day for better foot care.

Camp Etiquette

• Don't be late! Start out each session on a good foot. Be on time with all your equipment ready to go. Try not to yawn while the coaches are talking. Even if you are going on your 5th hour of camp and suffering from a severe case of sleep deprivation, try to resist the urge. If you absolutely have to yawn or cough make sure you cover your mouth.

• Don't chew gum! Enough said.

• Be courteous to other athletes. This is a great chance to develop camaraderie but still give your all in drills and play. Play hard but fair.

• Be respectful to the coaches and instructors. Do not get in the front row if you do not know the drill or exercise. Don't ever sit down or cross your arms. Always make sure you thank the coach at the end of each session.

Players don't get better from drills or practice. Those things reinforce talent. Players get better from game time experience. They learn how to react, to strategize, to set goals and to deliver when they are in the heat of a game. A great coach will let that happen. Very little gain comes from riding the bench. Except maybe a good dose of humility.

—Mary Yorke Oates
High School and Collegiate Athlete, Basketball and Field Hockey Coach, Former US Olympic Development Coach

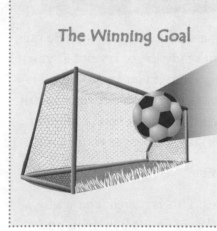

The Winning Goal

Attending summer camps and special coaching clinics in addition to your regular practices is one of the best ways to push yourself to the next level and become a stronger and more versatile athlete.

15. Surviving and Thriving as a Soccer Family

—Contributed by the Rogers Family—Rob, Genia,
Robert, Hunter and Anna

From the Father of an Athlete

The title of "Soccer Mom" may be prominent in today's society but the role of soccer father is also very important! Soccer games are exciting—you are exposed to all of the elements. It requires great athletic skill (speed, agility, and flexibility) and also a keen mind for strategy and field placement. There is a whole new vocabulary that comes with the game—offsides, head butts, penalty kicks, red cards, etc. Obviously, the playing rules will differ slightly depending on whether your child is playing recreational soccer or on a regional premier team. Following a few simple guidelines and recommendations will set you and your child up for success for practice, games and tournaments. The obvious ones, like arrive early and wear comfortable clothes, are just the beginning of setting the stage for success. This chapter will prepare you for the many other rules that require more experience and preparation.

> My heroes are and were my parents. I can't
> see having anyone else as my heroes.
>
> —Michael Jordan

Preparation for a game begins long before the game begins. Peak performance can be directly influenced by the habits of your child the day before their game. Make sure that your child stays active the day before a game but not so active that they push the muscles to an extreme. It is always good to stretch well and get the blood flowing in the legs throughout the course of the day. Make sure your child gets plenty of rest the night before and stays close to a sleep routine that is normal for an ordinary day at school. Plenty of rest, but not too much, can set your body up to perform at a high level when you have to call on it to excel. It is very important for your athlete to hydrate well several hours before competition begins. If it is an early morning game then ensure they get plenty of water the day before. Try to avoid waking your athlete up at the last minute and rushing them to the game.

The Day of the Game

Plan to arrive early because you will have to be sure your athlete has time to get mentally prepared and physically warmed up. One of the most common injuries in soccer is a torn hamstring because of the explosive moves associated with the quick kicks. Experiencing a thorough warm up will help to stretch and lengthen the muscle and prepare it for action. Typically the coaches will have the players warm up with a slow jog around the field followed by a series of stretches. Stretching cold muscles before a warm up is often the beginning of injury. The mental preparation of soccer is a significant part of the game. Try using the time the night before and the day of the game talking to your athlete about different game scenarios and how they might respond in each. You might talk about different strategies if they are ahead or behind on the scoreboard. Oftentimes in soccer, a match is decided by one goal. In tight games it is important to understand what to do and how to react to different competitive environments. These environments can be influenced by factors such as personalities from

Be very positive and make sure encouragement is your number one point of influence.

their teammates to the style of a referee to the energy and skill of an opposing team. There comes a time in most soccer games where the frustration mounts between competitors and it is very important to instruct your child to channel that frustration away from their opponent and onto their own abilities to excel. Redirecting this energy from a person to your own performance can sometimes give you that competitive edge that makes the difference between winning and losing. Unfortunately, you both may even need to prepare for adversarial comments from parents on the sidelines. If weather is extreme you will find it helpful to instruct your athlete about proper dress that provides both protection and freedom of movement. Anticipating the proper conditions will give your athlete a chance to move through the starts and stops of a game with maximum efficiency. Sometimes there are many miles traveled in the car to get to a game. On long rides you should make sure to stop frequently and allow your child to stretch their muscles and walk around a bit. This is just as true on the ride home after a long and hard game. Most athletes like to sleep in the car but this is when the muscles stiffen up and cramps set in. Make sure you get frequent stops both coming and going to ballgames. No one should jump right out of a car and onto the field of action if they have been sitting for an extended period. The car rides provide a good chance to reinforce a few key points for your child to focus on during the game. Don't overload them with details. Make sure their mind is clear and allow their natural tendencies to take control. Be very positive leading up to a game and make sure encouragement is your number one point of influence. You can never overemphasize how proud you are of your child and that, win or lose, nothing will ever change that. I love to tell my teams that doing their best is all I can ever ask of them.

From the Sidelines

Spending time with the other players on the team and their families is part of the enjoyment of the games. Getting to know names and jersey numbers helps you to be a great team supporter from the sideline. There is definitely a code of etiquette in the game of soccer similar to golf. Because parents are typically sitting very close to the field in lawn chairs or bleachers, comments from the sidelines should always be of a positive nature. The referees can hear all of the comments and yelling at him or her will only aggravate them and make it harder on your team! Your children will hear your voice as well—let them hear your words of encouragement, recognition of nice plays, and sometimes a quick reminder to keep their cool will pull them back from a hot head response to a shady play made by a competitor. Your child is going to recognize your behavior as a spectator. Make sure you are setting a great example by not arguing and by being very supportive of the game and those in authority over it. Be encouraging toward the coach and if you have any negative comments, address them specifically with the coach first. Never bring the conflict to the attention of the athlete. Let them focus solely on the playing of the game.

Bringing comfortable seats is a must. A chair with a carrying strap and a rolling cooler are definitely worth the investment. You will typically be hiking in from parking lots sometimes a half-mile away. The players and coaches are typically positioned on one side of the field and the spectators on the other side. Typically parents will line up across from their team's bench. Often however if you are sitting on the bleachers you will be sitting with the parents of the other team. Remember your manners! Sitting on field level will give you one angle of the play—but many parents enjoy sitting up on a hill for a different angle.

Get an experienced parent to explain the game rules to you. They can be complicated, especially at the higher levels of competition. Referencing local team Web sites for club teams will help you get familiar with the rules and regulations of play. The elimination process during tournament play is very complicated and differs from tournament to tournament. Trust me, your coaches will be on top of this—it may be, "If this team does that, then we have to do this, etc!"

Doing a little bit of homework will allow you to better participate in the process of the sport with your child. Many of the rules are complicated and your child may be confused and need you to guide him/her through the regulations. It is important to understand some of the major ones, such as what is "offsides."

Practice the *Rudy* philosophy

Years ago there was a football movie about a kid with little ability but lots of heart who stuck with his dream to play college football for Notre Dame. This true story, a movie called *Rudy*, helped me teach my child the best attitude to have when he was not getting the playing time he thought he deserved. I urged him and players I have coached to do what you can to help the team. Be positive, supportive of your teammates, work hard every day in practice and your time will come. Then I made him watch the movie. Also, as a parent, don't bad mouth the coach in front of your child or give support to his complaints about how bad the officiating was. Those too-easy targets are seldom the reasons for a bad outcome, and giving in to that sets a bad example for your child.

As the father of an athlete your number one role is support. Get involved. Be an assistant coach. Take pictures of everyone's kids. Put together a first aid kit and become the one the kids come to for a bandage or ice pack. You can be confident that the money you spend on sports is being put to good use. The sports world is teaching your child life skills and confidence. These athletes train and practice because they want to do well. They put their hearts into each event. With these rules and a little effort you will survive and thrive at their practices, games, and competitions. And just your being there will make all the difference in the world.

Notes from a Sports Mom

The best part of allowing your children to participate in athletics is the chance you have to watch them mature, gain new skills, and grow as people. The healthy atmosphere, the social time with friends, and the chance to contribute to a team effort are just some of the benefits. Whether your child is the "star" or the "chief bench warmer," your job is to show up, be there before and after the game and make sure that all experiences turn into an eventual positive one.

Here are some practical "Mom" tips that may save you from learning things the hard way:

• When playing in out of state tournaments or bad weather at home bringing a survival kit is a must. A blanket and seat cushion if sitting on the stadium seats and a comfortable chair for the sidelines.

• An umbrella or piece of plastic—some places do not allow umbrellas lest you drip all over the person seated next to you, but a large cut of polyethylene folds nicely in your pocket and can serve as a tent for the serious storms. Because at times, it is a driving rain, a strong golf type umbrella is best. It is also nice to shield you from the intense sun rays during summer/spring games.

• A towel or plastic bag—for your kid's muddy cleats and to protect your seats and carpet floorboards. I bought the hard plastic floorboard pieces for my Honda Pilot—the best $200 I have spent!

• Sunglasses with polarized filters—you really will see the action better with less glare and protect your eyes from ultraviolet light damage.

• Snacks—if you have younger children with you, packing a cooler is a must. Depending on where you play and the level that your child is playing, there may not be concessions available for regular games. Tournaments will typically have concession stands set up as well as public restrooms.

Our experience is that often the concessions are at a distant field and not reachable during the games. It never fails that your child will always score an amazing goal the moment you step away! The concessions typically do not have the healthiest of fare so we use them as a treat to celebrate the "win" after they have eaten the healthy snacks we brought.

• Cash. Your experience as a human ATM will come in handy here.

Prior to Game Day

• Have a family meeting to decide how much time and money can be devoted to athletics and how many sports each child can play. Soccer club fees can be very expensive and with the traveling teams the expense of hotels, gas, and meals can quickly add up. The primary equipment cost is in the cleats and shin guards. Because of the intensity of play—high quality cleats are a must. Common complaints are achy feet and shin splints from poor shoe choices. Warm clothing—turtlenecks, hats and gloves are a must for winter play, and warm ups for the players after play are helpful for injury prevention and catching colds.

• Help your child come up with a system to keep up with their uniforms, cleats, shin guards and socks. This is a huge source of stress if you are late and cannot find the things you need. Especially have a check list for tournaments—cleats (back up cleats if you have them), extra socks, all required uniforms, water bottles and healthy snacks.

- Drive to and from practices and games with your athlete as much as possible. We have amazing conversations on these car rides. Conversations shift from explaining the game strategy and rules to deeper important discussions about life. Be prepared to roll down your windows on the car ride home—soccer players have a unique fragrance to them!

- Try to eat healthy as a family, exercise, and manage stress in a proactive way. Keep the pantry and refrigerator stocked with lots of fruits and vegetables and whole grain snacks. Find time to take care of yourself. You must be a good role model for your athlete. Studies show the number one predictor of whether your children will grow up and have healthy habits is whether you model this for them.

- Most of all have fun and treasure every moment.

Younger Brother and Sister Survival Guide

—by Anna Rogers and Hunter Rogers

Ten Ways to Entertain Yourself at a Game or a Three-Day Tournament

If you are under 12 years old:

- Bring action figures/toy cars/or Barbie dolls.

- Make a fort out of the folding chairs and your parent's blankets.

- Bring a football/Frisbee/or soccer ball to play with on the next field or during half time.

- Eat something from the concession stand every hour or bring healthy snacks (get money from mom or dad).

- Bring your Game Boy.

- Bring your portable DVD player to watch a movie.

- Play with your mom's cell phone/call a friend.

- Talk your mom into letting you bring a friend.

- Play in the nearby sandbox or playground.

- Take a nap.

- Watch your sister or brother play.

- Tell her/him how great she/he did!

If you are over 12 years old:

- Bring an iPod or another way to listen to your own music.

- Play games on your cell phone or call a friend.

- Meet kids from other teams and schools.

- Bring homework and get ahead for the coming week.

- Bring your portable gaming system (remember to charge it before you leave home).

- Meet more girls/boys!

- Take a nap.

- Go for a hike in nearby woods or on the trails.

- Actually watch most of the game—you will win brownie points with your brother/sister and your parents.

- If you are in a new city for a tournament, research cool places that you can go to while waiting for the next games (climbing centers in the area, cool stadiums, aquariums, zoos). Your parents will be more likely to spend the money if you are being good on the sidelines. ☺

- If you can't beat them—join them!

The Winning Goal

Soccer is a family affair!

16. Life Lessons Gained through Soccer

—by a Young Athlete

Here are some things that I have learned through athletics that I believe will help me in life

Dedication—If you are serious about soccer, you commit your body, your mind, your time, and your energy to it. I have learned to devote my life to something I truly care about.

Confidence—To play and compete in front of your peers, family and community takes will and courage. This self-assurance will help me take new opportunities in the future without hesitation and will keep me from holding back.

Time Management—I have learned to make good use of time. If I have homework or something to do, I get it done efficiently because the faster it gets done, the more sleep I get.

Every kid around the world who plays soccer wants to be Pele. I have a great responsibility to show them not just how to be like a soccer player, but how to be like a man.

—Pele, Brazilian Soccer Star

Passion—For me, soccer is something that I can turn to for support. I can express myself without having to explain anything. It is an escape for me when everything else is going wrong. Once you have found a passion it becomes a base that you can always return to even if you are 45 years old and CEO of a company.

Perseverance—Sometimes on the last set of push-ups, sit-ups, or sprints you are not sure if you can do any more. Sound familiar? Participating in soccer has taught me to push myself farther than I ever thought possible. I now know that when I reach a point in life when most people would just give up, I can continue to fight and push myself to my limit.

The list of things I learned from playing soccer is endless. Where do I start? Soccer and sports in general have done so much for me that I have ultimately built my life around them. It is a way of life and now I'm giving a little of my life experiences in sports back by teaching and coaching. Some of the most important concepts I've grasped through sports include time management, how to practice and plan for the future, dedication, discipline, commitment, accountability, drive, determination, the importance of rest, proper diet, politics, handling upsets with grace, handling success with grace, and stress management.

You don't always agree with the people you work with or for and the way you get the job done is not always pretty.

You are what you eat and drink.

Drink more water.

—Lauren B. Lukowski, MS
Soccer Coach and Teacher at The Howard School, Semi-Pro
Player, Physical Educator, MS in Sport Health Science

Sacrifice—In order to train and do well in school I have had to sacrifice many things. The amount of sleep I get, my social life with school friends, and being involved in multiple activities such as my school's musical or playing another sport are all affected by my commitment to one sport. But that is a decision I have made and I am okay with it. In fact it is a true test of how far you are willing to go and how much you are willing to sacrifice. You might want to play several sports or you might want to focus on soccer year round. Think seriously about your goal and then arrange your schedule so you can achieve that goal. Being able to prioritize in your life is an important life skill.

I want all of my students involved in our school sports program. One of the primary components of athletics for students is to provide them with healthy social interactions in a positive peer group. Kids will find a peer group—I want to be sure that that group has a healthy focus and is led by good role models. I am proud that we also promote "winning with class" and "losing with dignity"—great life lessons to foster resilience and good character.

—Debbie Lamm, Head of the Middle School at Charlotte Latin School (Also a former bench warmer on a high school, championship volleyball team)

Leadership—One of the best ways to get better at soccer is to watch those who are older and have more experience than you. I learned so much from watching these older role models and now that I am the oldest, I can be a role model myself. Choose a team or club program where the coaches are people you can look up to as well. Sometimes you are with them for more hours than you are with your own parents. Your coaches and fellow athletes become part of your family and you benefit from these relationships. Respecting and learning from my role models has taught me how to be a leader.

The Winning Goal

It is important for everyone to find something they are passionate about. That dedication and commitment will teach and reinforce many skills needed for a happy and healthy life. A few of us might actually become professional soccer players. That is great but probably won't last forever. You will still need all of these life skills to deal with your success in a positive way.

About the Author

Toni Branner is director of Fitness Concepts, Inc., and teaches on topics such as anti-aging, children's wellness, motivation for lifestyle change, whole food nutrition, stress management and safe exercise.

Toni received her Master's Degree in Exercise Physiology from the University of North Carolina at Chapel Hill where she also served as director of the UNC Employee Health and Fitness Center and as a faculty member in the Department of Physical Education, Exercise and Sports Science.

Branner has authored four previous books. *The Safe Exercise Handbook (5th Edition)* promotes the importance of a regular exercise program as a means of improving your health and quality of life. This book is used on US Navy aircraft carriers to guide military personnel through their workouts. *Wilby's Fitness Book,* includes innovative ideas to help children stay healthy and feel good about themselves. *Care & Feeding of a Dancer* and *Care & Feeding of an Athlete* are two other books in the Care & Feeding series.

Through fitness classes for children and adults, as well as numerous speaking engagements, workshops and academic presentations, Toni has shown thousands of people the way to perform effective, injury-free fitness and achieve maximal health.

Recommended Resources

The Care and Feeding of a Soccer Player Resource List is available at:

www.thecareandfeedingof.us

Up-to-date lists of camps, equipment, books, magazines, Web site links, private coaches, and more.

Author Information:
Toni Tickel Branner, MA
Exercise Physiologist, Wellness Consultant, Physical Educator, Professional Speaker

Professional Speaking, Workshops, and Seminars on Fitness, Nutrition and Stress Management

The Care and Feeding of a Soccer Player for Parents and Athletes

The Care and Feeding of a Soccer Player Free E-Updates

The Care and Feeding of an Athlete Seminars for Parents and Athletes

The Care and Feeding of an Athlete Free E-Updates

The Care and Feeding of a Dancer Studio Seminar for Parents and Students

The Care and Feeding of a Dancer Free E-Updates

Health Made Simple Free E-Updates for people interested in general health, fitness and nutrition

Contact Toni at: Fitness Concepts

Website: *www.tonibranner.com*
Email: *tonibranner@aol.com*
Phone: (704) 551-9051

Books and Resources by Toni T. Branner, MA

The Care and Feeding of a Soccer Player by Toni T. Branner

The Care and Feeding of an Athlete by Toni T. Branner

The Care and Feeding of a Dancer by Toni T. Branner

Wilby's Fitness Book by Toni T. Branner

The Safe Exercise Handbook and Workout DVD with upper body and lower body exercise bands by Toni T. Branner (*www.tonibranner.com*)

Recommended Books for Soccer Athletes and Parents

Sports Success Rx! by Paul R. Stricker, MD
(*www.aap.org/parenting books*)

Dr. Sears' LEAN Kids
by William Sears, MD and Peter Sears, MD

PowerPack for the Winning Edge
by Roy Vartabedian, PhD and Jack Medina, MA

The China Study by T. Colin Campbell

Prevent and Reverse Heart Disease
by Caldwell B. Esselstyn Jr., MD

Eat More, Weigh Less by Dean Ornish, MD

The Omega-3 Connection by Andrew L. Stoll, MD

Digestive Tune-Up by John A. McDougall, MD

Dr. Neal Barnard's Program for Reversing Diabetes by Neal D. Barnard, MD

Hungry for Health by Susan Silberstein, PhD

Recommended Web sites and Newsletters

Paul Stricker MD Web site *www.drpaulstricker.com*

American Council on Exercise *www.acefitness.org*

American Heart Association *www.americanheart.org*

American Dietetic Association *www.eatright.org*

American College of Sports Medicine *www.acsm.org*

American College of Cardiology *www.acc.org*

American Cancer Society *www.cancer.org*

Fruit and Veggie Info and Recipes *www.5aday.com*

Center for Advancement in Cancer Education *www.beatcancer.org*

Nutrition information unbiased by industry *www.pcrm.org*

The Wellness Forum *www.wellnessforum.com*

Dept. of Agriculture site for families and children *www.mypyramid.gov*

Fruit and Veggie Info and Recipes *www.vegweb.com*

Bill Sears, MD Wellness Web site *www.askdrsears.com*

Product Recommendations

Fitness Equipment

For fairly priced, high quality fitness equipment, weights, mats, stability balls, videos, etc.

Fitness Wholesale: (888) FWO-RDER or *fitnesswholesale.com*

For Juice Plus+® Whole Food Nutrition Products

Juice Plus+® provides the nutritional essence of 17 different fruits, vegetables, and grains in convenient and inexpensive capsule form.

For information and research

Go to: *www.juiceplus.com* or call (800) 347-6350

(Children between the ages of 6 and 15 years are eligible to take Juice Plus+® for free for up to three years as part of the Children's Health Study if one adult takes the capsules.)

For Juice Plus+ Complete® Smoothie Mix

We recommend this product because it is plant-based protein and is perfect for breakfast or for replacing glycogen in the muscles after games or practice. It is high in calcium, vitamin D, phytonutrients and fiber.

Comes in French Vanilla, Dutch Chocolate, and Variety Pack.

Go to: *www.juiceplus.com* or call (800) 347-6350

For hundreds of resources for athletes, or to sign up for free newsletters go to

www.thecareandfeedingof.us

Please contact me with feedback and comments on the material in this book. I would love to hear from you and visit your team or school sometime. The best to you and your family and keep playing!

—Sincerely, Toni Branner